STARSEEDS AND COSMIC ALIGNMENTS

Galactic Origins and Earthly Missions

Campbell Quinn McCarthy

S.D.N Publishing

Copyright © 2023 S.D.N Publishing

All rights reserved

The characters and events portrayed in this book are fictitious. Any similarity to real persons, living or dead, is coincidental and not intended by the author.

No part of this book may be reproduced, or stored in a retrieval system, or transmitted in any form or by any means, electronic, mechanical, photocopying, recording, or otherwise, without express written permission of the publisher.

ISBN: 9798860127555

CONTENTS

Title Page
Copyright
General Disclaimer   1
Chapter 1: Historical Accounts: Star Beings in Ancient Texts   3
Chapter 2: Galactic Origins: Different Star Systems Explored   7
Chapter 3: Identifying Marks: Traits of a Starseed   10
Chapter 4: Earthly Missions: Starseed Roles and Responsibilities   14
Chapter 5: Cosmic Alignments: Understanding Planetary Shifts   18
Chapter 6: The Awakening Process: Remembering Galactic Heritage   22
Chapter 7: Healing Modalities for Starseeds   25
Chapter 8: Earth as a School: Lessons and Karmic Ties   28
Chapter 9: Interstellar Communication: Connecting with Star Families   32
Chapter 10: Starseeds and Ascension: The Journey to 5D   35
Chapter 11: Twin Flames and Soul Groups: Galactic Relationships   39
Chapter 12: Navigating Earthly Challenges: Starseed Struggles   43
Chapter 13: Tools and Crystals: Amplifying Starseed   46

Energies

Chapter 14: Starseeds in the New Age: Modern Roles and Activations — 50

Chapter 15: Toward the Future: Starseeds in the Cosmic Evolution — 54

Chapter 16: Chakras and Energy Centers: Starseed Anatomy — 57

Chapter 17: Divination and Signs: Guidance for Starseeds — 60

Chapter 18: Starseeds and Ecology: Guardians of the Earth — 64

Chapter 19: Activating DNA: The Science Behind Starseeds — 68

Chapter 20: Starseed Children: Indigos, Crystals, and Rainbows — 72

Chapter 21: Starseed Symbols and Codes — 76

Chapter 22: Channeling and Mediumship: Accessing Higher Realms — 79

Chapter 23: The Law of One and Starseeds — 83

Chapter 24: Famous Starseeds: Real-life Examples — 87

Chapter 25: Galactic Languages and Light Codes — 91

Chapter 26: Sacred Geometry: The Blueprint of Creation — 94

Chapter 27: Soul Contracts and Free Will: The Starseed Dilemma — 98

Chapter 28: Starseeds and Earth's History — 102

Chapter 29: Wanderers and Walk-ins: Other Types of Starseeds — 105

Chapter 30: Lightworkers vs. Starseeds: Similarities and Differences — 109

Chapter 31: Starseeds and Spiritual Traditions — 113

Chapter 32: The Shadow Side: Pitfalls and Misconceptions — 117

Chapter 33: Integration: Living a Balanced Starseed Life — 120

Chapter 34: Starseeds and Global Transformation — 124

Chapter 35: Conclusion: The Cosmic Journey Ahead — 128

THE END

GENERAL DISCLAIMER

This book is intended to provide general information to the reader on the topics covered. The author and publisher have made every effort to ensure that the information herein is accurate and up-to-date at the time of publication. However, they do not warrant or guarantee the accuracy, completeness, adequacy, or currency of the information contained in this book. The author and publisher expressly disclaim any liability or responsibility for any errors or omissions in the content herein.

The information, guidance, advice, tips, and suggestions provided in this book are not intended to replace professional advice or consultation. Readers are strongly encouraged to consult with an appropriate professional for specific advice tailored to their situation before making any decisions or taking any actions based on the content of this book.

The views and opinions expressed in this book are those of the author and do not necessarily reflect the official policy or position of any other agency, organization, employer or company.

The author and publisher are not responsible for any actions taken or not taken by the reader based on the information, advice, or suggestions provided in this book. The reader is solely responsible for their actions and the consequences thereof.

This book is not intended to be a source of legal, business, medical or psychological advice, and readers are cautioned to seek the services of a competent professional in these or other areas of expertise.

All product names, logos, and brands are property of their respective owners. All company, product and service names used in this book are for identification purposes only. Use of these names, logos, and brands does not imply endorsement.

Readers of this book are advised to do their own due diligence when it comes to making decisions and all information, products, services and advice that have been provided should be independently verified by your own qualified professionals.

By reading this book, you agree that the author and publisher are not responsible for your success or failure resulting from any information presented in this book.

CHAPTER 1: HISTORICAL ACCOUNTS: STAR BEINGS IN ANCIENT TEXTS

The notion of starseeds—souls believed to originate from other star systems, incarnated on Earth for special missions—can feel like a concept from modern New Age spirituality. Yet, if we go into ancient writings and religious scriptures, we can uncover stories and descriptions that have a striking similarity to what we now refer to as starseeds or star beings. In this chapter, we will examine how ancient texts like the Vedas, the Bible, and Sumerian cuneiform writings talk about celestial entities and how these accounts may align with the modern understanding of starseeds.

The Vedas and Cosmic Entities

The Vedas are ancient Indian scriptures written in Sanskrit, dated to approximately 1500–500 BCE. These texts contain hymns, philosophical discussions, and rituals, but they also reference a variety of celestial beings known as "Devas" and "Asuras." Devas are often considered divine entities associated with natural forces and cosmic events, whereas Asuras are usually depicted as beings of immense power but are not always aligned with divine virtues.

In the Rigveda, one of the four Vedas, there are mentions of celestial chariots known as "Vimanas," which were said to be vehicles of the gods. These Vimanas are described as flying objects that traversed the sky, sometimes even venturing between different realms. The advanced technology attributed to Vimanas and the celestial origin of Devas and Asuras might hint at beings with otherworldly or interstellar origins, reminiscent of the modern concept of starseeds.

Biblical Celestial Messengers

The Bible, the religious text foundational to Judaism and Christianity, also contains accounts of celestial entities, most notably angels. These heavenly messengers serve as intermediaries between the divine and the human realm, often delivering messages or performing miracles. In the book of Ezekiel, for example, the prophet describes seeing "four living creatures" with multiple wings and faces, each accompanied by a "wheel within a wheel" that moved along with them. Some interpret this vision as a form of ancient contact with celestial or even extraterrestrial beings.

Angels themselves are often described as beings of light, and in certain accounts like the Transfiguration of Jesus in the New Testament, there are instances where human figures transform into radiant beings. While the mainstream religious interpretation doesn't necessarily place these entities as originating from other star systems, the descriptions do resonate with some characteristics attributed to starseeds, such as beings of light with a mission to aid or enlighten humanity.

Sumerian Cuneiform Writings and the Annunaki

Sumerian civilization, one of the earliest known civilizations, had its own complex system of mythology and beliefs recorded in cuneiform script on clay tablets. Among the most intriguing are the stories of the Annunaki, a group of deities who descended from the sky to Earth. According to these ancient texts, the Annunaki were responsible for imparting knowledge and possibly even genetic material to humans, contributing to our advancement.

The Sumerian accounts have been the subject of much debate and interpretation, especially among those who propose ancient astronaut theories. Though not universally accepted, the notion that the Annunaki could be beings from another star system aligns with the starseed concept of souls incarnated from different celestial origins with a mission to influence Earth's development.

Relevance to Modern Starseed Concepts

While the ancient texts discussed here are embedded in their own cultural and religious contexts, their accounts of celestial beings resonate with the current understanding of starseeds. The beings described in these scriptures often come from other realms or skies, possess advanced knowledge or abilities, and interact with humans in ways that influence our spiritual or material progress.

It's crucial to note that the connections made between ancient texts and the starseed concept are interpretive and speculative. The ancient Vedas, Biblical stories, and Sumerian tablets were not explicitly discussing starseeds as understood today. However, these age-old narratives do contribute to a broader, archetypal understanding of celestial influence on human life, offering a form of "historical precedent" for contemporary starseed ideas.

In summary, the concept of celestial beings influencing human life is not new and can be traced back to some of the oldest religious and spiritual texts known to us. Whether these accounts offer glimpses of what we now call starseeds, or simply contribute to the rich tapestry of humanity's collective mythos, they do provide intriguing parallels that inspire further exploration and thought.

CHAPTER 2: GALACTIC ORIGINS: DIFFERENT STAR SYSTEMS EXPLORED

In our journey to understand the enigmatic and fascinating realm of starseeds, it is essential to delve into their galactic origins. According to various esoteric teachings and spiritual philosophies, starseeds are believed to originate from multiple star systems, each carrying its own set of unique characteristics, wisdom, and missions. In this chapter, we will explore some of the prominent star systems, such as the Pleiades, Arcturus, and Sirius, which are often cited as the celestial homes of starseeds.

Pleiades: The Seven Sisters

The Pleiades, often referred to as the "Seven Sisters," is an open star cluster located in the constellation of Taurus. Ancient cultures, ranging from the Greeks to Native Americans, have revered this star cluster for its beauty and mystical significance. Starseeds originating from Pleiades are commonly termed "Pleiadians." Pleiadians are thought to be compassionate, empathetic, and concerned with healing and nurturing the Earth. They are often described as emotionally intelligent and are deeply connected to nature. The wisdom imparted by Pleiadians is often related to spirituality, community-building, and fostering emotional well-being.

Arcturus: The Shepherd Star

One of the brightest stars seen in the night sky, Arcturus may be found in the Bootes constellation. In the realm of starseeds, beings originating from this star are known as "Arcturians." Often cited as some of the oldest souls in our galaxy, they are considered to be highly advanced in terms of technology and spirituality. Arcturians are thought to focus on intellectual development and are often associated with innovations in science and technology on Earth. It is said that they emit a frequency that promotes healing and that they are concerned with dimensional shifts. Their goal is to assist humanity in ascending to higher planes of consciousness.

Sirius: The Dog Star

Sirius, which is a member of the Canis Major constellation, is the brightest star visible from Earth's surface at night. Starseeds from Sirius, often referred to as "Sirians," are considered to be focused on spiritual enlightenment and ascension. They are credited with bringing ancient wisdom to Earth, including early foundations for astrology, alchemy, and even Gnostic spiritual beliefs. Sirians are often drawn to the metaphysical and esoteric, dedicating themselves to disciplines that offer deeper insights into the universe and our place within it. They are also believed to have a keen interest in Earth's ancient civilizations, particularly those that had insights into celestial events.

Other Star Systems

While Pleiades, Arcturus, and Sirius are among the most commonly cited, there are various other star systems like

Andromeda, Lyra, and Orion, which are also believed to be origins for different starseeds. Each star system carries its own unique frequencies and mission agendas, adding to the rich tapestry of starseed diversity.

Multiple Origins and Hybrid Souls

It's also essential to note that some starseeds are thought to have multiple origins, indicating that their souls have journeyed through various star systems, collecting a plethora of cosmic wisdom and traits along the way. These are often termed as "hybrid souls" and are believed to have a broader range of missions on Earth, often combining the tasks and wisdom of multiple star systems.

Summary

The concept of starseeds' galactic origins serves as a vibrant palette of cosmic diversity. From the empathetic and nurturing Pleiadians to the intellectually advanced Arcturians and spiritually enlightened Sirians, each group brings its own unique gifts and challenges to the earthly experience. Understanding these origins is not merely an esoteric exercise but a way to better understand the different missions and qualities starseeds are believed to bring to our planet. It sets the stage for appreciating the full scope of their contributions to Earth's evolution and lays the foundation for deeper exploration into the complexities of their missions, traits, and responsibilities.

CHAPTER 3: IDENTIFYING MARKS: TRAITS OF A STARSEED

Introduction

The notion that starseeds possess unique traits—be it behavioral, psychological, or even physical—provides a captivating dimension to the broader starseed narrative. This chapter delves into the diverse characteristics commonly associated with starseeds, shedding light on what sets them apart from the general populace. Keep in mind that these traits are culled from anecdotal reports, spiritual traditions, and metaphysical texts. Scientific evidence supporting these attributes is limited.

Behavioral Traits

Empathy and Compassion

One of the most commonly cited characteristics of starseeds is a heightened sense of empathy and compassion towards other beings. This heightened emotional sensitivity often extends beyond humans to animals and the natural world. Starseeds are often deeply moved by social issues, seeking to engage in activities that alleviate suffering and foster well-being.

Drive for Purpose

Starseeds usually display an overwhelming sense of purpose or mission from an early age. This isn't merely ambition; it is a yearning for meaningful engagement with the world. Starseeds often question the established norms of society, rejecting materialistic values in favor of spiritual or humanitarian goals.

Psychological Traits

Intuition and Psychic Abilities

Starseeds frequently report having strong intuitive or psychic abilities. Whether it's an uncanny knack for reading people or having premonitions, these psychic tendencies often manifest early in life. This perceived direct line to universal wisdom could serve as a guiding light for their earthly missions.

Sense of Alienation

A pervasive sense of being 'different' or not belonging is another typical psychological trait. Despite being compassionate and often sociable, starseeds can feel like outsiders, as if they are tuned to a different frequency than the rest of the world. This could manifest as a sense of loneliness or a longing for a 'home' they can't quite define.

Physical Traits

Distinctive Eyes

Some anecdotal accounts suggest that starseeds possess

unusually captivating eyes. The eyes are described as being large, intense, and often, older than their years—imbued with a wisdom or knowing that can be unsettling or deeply comforting, depending on the observer.

Unusual Birthmarks

Although this is more contentious, there are accounts that suggest starseeds may have distinctive birthmarks or physical peculiarities that set them apart. These marks are sometimes seen as symbolic connections to their galactic origins, although interpretations vary widely.

Health Sensitivities

Starseeds are often reported to have heightened sensitivities to their environment, which could include anything from a susceptibility to food intolerances, to being particularly sensitive to energies and emotional climates. These sensitivities, while at times challenging, are also believed to enhance their intuitive and empathic capabilities.

Unique Skill Sets

Many starseeds display a natural affinity for certain skill sets that align with their purported missions on Earth. For example, some may find themselves drawn to healing professions, while others excel in creative fields, technology, or social activism. These skill sets, often developed with little formal training, provide them with the tools to enact their envisioned purposes.

Summary

While no single trait can definitively identify someone as a starseed, a combination of these characteristics often serves as a compelling indicator. From behavioral and psychological markers like heightened empathy and a relentless drive for purpose, to physical traits and unique sensitivities, starseeds appear to navigate the world somewhat differently. These idiosyncratic traits not only add layers of complexity to their individual personalities but also equip them for the specialized missions they are believed to carry out on Earth. As the quest for understanding the starseed phenomenon continues, these traits provide intriguing waypoints in the exploration of their earthly lives and cosmic origins.

CHAPTER 4: EARTHLY MISSIONS: STARSEED ROLES AND RESPONSIBILITIES

The concept of starseeds—souls believed to have origins in distant star systems and incarnated on Earth for specific missions—has captivated the minds of many in spiritual communities. While previous chapters have discussed their galactic origins and distinguishing traits, this chapter focuses on understanding the roles and responsibilities that starseeds are said to have here on Earth. These roles range from spiritual guidance to practical innovation across various fields. Let's delve into this fascinating facet of starseed lore.

Spiritual Teachers and Guides

One of the most commonly cited roles for starseeds is that of spiritual teachers or guides. The idea is that starseeds, with their unique perspectives and heightened sensitivities, are naturally inclined to guide others in their spiritual journeys. Their teachings are often characterized by an emphasis on universal love, compassion, and the interconnectedness of all beings. In some cases, starseeds who are spiritual guides may not be overtly spiritual in their presentation, but they still subtly inspire and uplift those around them, promoting positive change and greater understanding.

Innovators and Visionaries

Starseeds are sometimes said to be ahead of their time, with knowledge or insights that may not yet be recognized or accepted by the general populace. This is a popular descriptor of a starseed. In this capacity, individuals have the potential to play an innovative role in a variety of sectors, including but not limited to science, technology, medicine, and social justice. Their innate creativity and unconventional thinking allow them to envision solutions to problems that others may not see. Some believe that starseeds who are innovators often work in areas that align with their larger mission of uplifting humanity and aiding in its evolution.

Environmental Guardians

Another important role for starseeds is that of guardians of the Earth. They are often deeply connected to the planet and feel a strong urge to protect it. This can manifest in various ways—through environmental activism, sustainable living, or research that aims to solve ecological challenges. Their commitment to planetary well-being goes hand-in-hand with their broader cosmic missions, making them dedicated stewards of both Earth and the larger cosmos.

Healers and Empaths

Many starseeds are said to possess strong healing abilities, both in traditional and alternative forms of medicine. Their empathic abilities allow them to sense the emotional and physical needs of others, providing them with unique insights into the healing process. Starseeds with these qualities often find themselves drawn to fields like healthcare, counseling, or alternative therapies like Reiki and sound healing. Their work often transcends the physical plane, as they are believed to work with energy fields and auras to promote holistic well-being.

Catalysts for Change

In a more generalized sense, starseeds can act as catalysts for change in the lives of individuals or even entire communities. By merely being themselves—by radiating their unique energies—they inspire change in others. They often question established norms and encourage others to do the same, fostering an environment where new ideas can flourish. Whether it's through their friendships, family relationships, or larger communal roles, they stimulate growth and transformation.

Interconnected Missions

It's crucial to note that these roles are not mutually exclusive. A single starseed may embody multiple roles over their lifetime or even simultaneously. The underlying thread through all these roles is the idea of service—service to humanity, to the planet, and to the broader cosmic mission that they are believed to be a part of. Each role serves as a different expression of this overarching mission, adapted to the specific circumstances and challenges they encounter in their earthly lives.

In summary, starseeds are often seen as multifaceted beings with a range of roles and responsibilities on Earth, from spiritual guides and teachers to innovators in various domains. Through these roles, they contribute to both earthly and cosmic evolutions, aligning their actions with a broader mission of universal upliftment and growth. Whether you identify as a starseed or are intrigued by the concept, understanding these roles can offer you a richer perspective on the unique contributions these fascinating souls make to our world.

CHAPTER 5: COSMIC ALIGNMENTS: UNDERSTANDING PLANETARY SHIFTS

Astrological and astronomical phenomena have long been subjects of fascination, often interwoven into the cultural, spiritual, and philosophical fabrics of various civilizations. For starseeds—those who believe they are souls incarnated from other star systems—cosmic alignments and planetary shifts hold special significance. These celestial events are thought to impact starseeds uniquely, serving as cosmic triggers for awakening, growth, and alignment with their earthly missions. In this chapter, we will delve into the nature of these cosmic occurrences and explore how they may affect starseeds' lives and objectives.

Eclipses: The Dance of Shadows

Eclipses, both lunar and solar, are often viewed as powerful transformational periods. During an eclipse, the Earth, Sun, and Moon align in a unique geometric relationship. This alignment is not just a stunning spectacle; many believe it has energetic repercussions. In astrological circles, eclipses are often associated with fate or destiny, presenting pivotal points in individual life paths.

For starseeds, eclipses can act as cosmic recalibration events. The shadow play of these celestial bodies may signify inner shifts and periods of introspection. Starseeds may find themselves pondering on their earthly roles more deeply during these times, or even experiencing profound revelations that help align them with their missions. They may feel an intensified connection to their star families or find it easier to access other forms of cosmic wisdom.

Solstices and Equinoxes: The Rhythms of Earth

Solstices and equinoxes mark the changing seasons and are among the most anciently observed celestial events. Solstices occur when the Sun reaches its highest or lowest point in the sky, signifying the longest and shortest days of the year. Equinoxes, on the other hand, occur when day and night are approximately of equal length.

For starseeds, these are potent times for energy work and spiritual practices. They may find themselves more attuned to the energies of the Earth and cosmos during these periods. Solstices and equinoxes could offer heightened opportunities for meditation, dream work, or intuitive insights, providing a natural setting for starseeds to align their energies with both their earthly environment and cosmic origins.

Planetary Alignments: Cosmic Synchronicities

Beyond eclipses and solstices, various planetary alignments like conjunctions, oppositions, and retrogrades are also considered significant. These alignments involve unique positions of planets in relation to Earth and each other. In astrology, such phenomena are believed to influence individual and collective experiences.

Starseeds often regard planetary alignments as windows of opportunity for various forms of growth, learning, and self-discovery. The energetic influences of these alignments may resonate differently with starseeds, often triggering inner transformations or revealing hidden insights that pertain to their missions. Some starseeds may find that these cosmic events activate latent abilities or deepen their intuitive senses, allowing them a clearer understanding of their roles on Earth.

Cosmic Cycles: Longer Timeframes

Starseeds also pay attention to longer cosmic cycles, such as the 26,000-year Precession of the Equinoxes or the more expansive Yugas in Hindu cosmology. These lengthy cycles are considered to offer broader perspectives on human evolution and consciousness shifts. For starseeds, understanding these long-term cycles is akin to grasping the 'bigger picture' of their collective mission. It helps place their individual experiences and challenges within a more expansive cosmic context.

The Cosmic Web: Interconnected Influences

While each type of cosmic event holds its unique influence, it's essential to recognize that they don't operate in isolation. The cosmos functions as an intricate web of interconnected influences. For starseeds, being attuned to these various celestial rhythms can offer a holistic understanding of their earthly journey. By respecting the unique energy each event brings, starseeds can better navigate their missions, learning to ebb and flow with the cosmic tides that shape not just their lives but the evolution of consciousness itself.

In summary, cosmic alignments and planetary shifts are more than just fascinating celestial events for starseeds; they serve as pivotal markers in their earthly journey. From the immediacy of eclipses to the grand sweep of cosmic cycles, these events offer starseeds unique opportunities for growth, self-discovery, and alignment with their cosmic missions. By understanding and integrating the energies of these cosmic phenomena, starseeds not only enrich their individual experiences but also contribute to the larger cosmic tapestry of which they are an integral part.

CHAPTER 6: THE AWAKENING PROCESS: REMEMBERING GALACTIC HERITAGE

The awakening process is a crucial juncture in the life of a starseed, an event—or sometimes a series of events—that triggers an intense internal shift. This shift leads to a heightened awareness of one's galactic heritage and a more profound understanding of their earthly mission. Many aspects contribute to this intricate process, and in this chapter, we'll explore some of the core elements that mark the awakening journey for starseeds.

The Triggering Event

Often, the awakening process begins with a triggering event that catalyzes deep introspection and questioning. This event may be a life crisis, an encounter with a spiritual mentor, or even a seemingly mundane experience imbued with unusual emotional or mental resonance. The triggering event essentially serves as a catalyst, nudging the starseed out of their comfort zone and compelling them to look within and question their existing beliefs and perceptions.

The Role of Intuition

Post the triggering event, the role of intuition becomes increasingly significant. Starseeds often report a heightened sense of intuition that guides them through their awakening. They may start to trust their inner guidance more readily and find themselves attracted to specific philosophies, texts, or spiritual practices that align with their newfound awareness. Some describe this phase as reconnecting with an innate "inner knowing" that had been suppressed or ignored in the past.

Synchronicities and Signs

Another hallmark of the awakening process is the frequent occurrence of synchronicities—meaningful coincidences that seem too purposeful to be mere chance. These synchronicities may come in various forms: seeing repetitive numbers, meeting people who profoundly influence their journey, or stumbling upon literature or teachings that resonate deeply with their emerging self-awareness. These coincidental events often serve as affirmations, reassuring starseeds that they are on the right path.

Expansion of Consciousness

As the awakening process unfolds, starseeds may experience an expansion of consciousness. This expansion is often accompanied by a greater acceptance of esoteric teachings and a heightened awareness of cosmic realities. Some report experiencing profound spiritual encounters or receiving intuitive insights that deepen their understanding of their galactic origins and earthly missions. This expansion of consciousness not only fosters spiritual growth but also impacts their daily life, relationships, and even their perspective on global issues.

Emotional and Physical Changes

The awakening process isn't solely a mental or spiritual endeavor; it often brings about significant emotional and sometimes physical changes. Emotional sensitivities may be amplified, leading to deeper empathy but also to greater vulnerability. Some starseeds find themselves undergoing physical changes as well, such as alterations in sleep patterns, dietary preferences, and even increased sensitivity to environmental factors like light and sound.

Challenges and Integration

Awakening is not a seamless process; it comes with its set of challenges. The dismantling of previously held beliefs can be unsettling, and the influx of new insights may create cognitive dissonance. Moreover, not everyone in a starseed's social circle may understand or support this profound internal shift, leading to potential conflicts or feelings of isolation. Therefore, the phase of integration is crucial, where the starseed finds a way to harmonize their expanded awareness with their earthly existence, possibly involving lifestyle changes, setting new boundaries, or seeking out like-minded communities for support.

In summary, the awakening process for starseeds is a complex and deeply individual journey, marked by triggering events, intuitive guidance, synchronicities, expanded consciousness, and both emotional and physical changes. While the journey involves its set of challenges, it also opens the doorway to a more authentic and purpose-driven life, allowing starseeds to align more closely with their galactic heritage and earthly missions. This awakening is not just a one-time event but an ongoing process, one that continues to unfold as starseeds navigate their unique paths in both the cosmic and earthly realms.

CHAPTER 7: HEALING MODALITIES FOR STARSEEDS

In the journey of life as a starseed, balancing one's galactic heritage with earthly experiences often requires an array of tools and practices, especially in the domain of healing. Many starseeds feel drawn to alternative healing modalities that resonate with their unique energetic makeup. This chapter explores some of those healing methods, including Reiki, sound healing, and crystal therapy, which have been reported as particularly effective for starseeds.

Reiki and Energy Healing

The Japanese art of Reiki is a type of energy healing that focuses on channeling the energy of the universal life force in order to increase one's whole physical, mental, and spiritual well-being. Starseeds often find this modality appealing because it aligns with their understanding of energy dynamics and interconnectedness. The concept of life force energy, or "Chi" in some traditions, complements the starseed's innate understanding of cosmic energy. Through Reiki, practitioners can balance the chakras, dissolve energy blocks, and thereby enable a smoother flow of cosmic information and guidance. Moreover, Reiki can serve as a way for starseeds to channel healing energies not only for themselves but also for the planet, resonating with their overarching mission of global transformation.

Sound Healing

Another avenue that has proven effective for many starseeds is sound healing. The principle behind this practice is that everything in the universe is in a state of vibration, including the cells in the human body. Sound healing, often conducted using Tibetan bowls, gongs, or tuning forks, harnesses the power of sound frequencies to bring about healing and transformation. Starseeds might feel particularly in tune with sound healing due to their resonance with universal harmonies and frequencies. The vibrations can affect the energetic body, attune the chakras, and even influence DNA, aligning well with the starseed's quest for awakening and activating dormant potentials.

Crystal Therapy

Crystals have long been valued for their healing properties and their ability to amplify energies. Starseeds, who are often sensitive to energy, may find the use of crystals in healing practices especially beneficial. Each type of crystal has its own unique properties; for instance, amethyst is commonly used for spiritual protection, while rose quartz is associated with love and compassion. By strategically placing these crystals on the body's energy centers or carrying them as personal talismans, starseeds can optimize their energy fields for their earthly missions and spiritual growth. Additionally, crystals can serve as a tangible link to a starseed's star home, creating a feeling of cosmic interconnectedness.

Shamanic Practices

Although not as mainstream as Reiki or crystal therapy, some starseeds are drawn to the ancient practice of shamanism.

Shamanic journeys, which often involve guided meditations, drumming, and sometimes plant-based medicines, can facilitate deep inner transformations. These practices often enable starseeds to explore other dimensions, reconnect with their star families, and receive direct insights into their earthly missions. This modality is potent but should be approached with care and preferably under the guidance of a trained and ethical practitioner.

Personalizing Your Healing Journey

While the healing modalities mentioned above have been found effective for many, it's essential for each starseed to personalize their healing journey. This could mean combining several methods or incorporating other practices like yoga, meditation, or breathwork that resonate on a personal level. When dealing with any kind of medical ailment, it is strongly recommended to speak with a qualified medical practitioner. Nevertheless, these alternative modalities have the potential to function as supplementary practices, which will enhance the starseed's overall well-being.

In summary, the realm of alternative healing offers various paths that can be particularly effective for starseeds. Whether it is channeling life force energy through Reiki, aligning vibrations via sound healing, harnessing the power of crystals, or journeying through shamanic practices, these methods offer unique benefits tailored to the starseed's energetic makeup. By embracing these practices, starseeds not only foster their own well-being but also contribute to the larger healing journey of the planet.

CHAPTER 8: EARTH AS A SCHOOL: LESSONS AND KARMIC TIES

The notion that Earth serves as a sort of cosmic classroom is not new. It has been part of spiritual traditions and philosophies for centuries. For starseeds, the idea holds particular resonance. They see Earth as a place where they can engage in essential life lessons and karmic exchanges. This chapter delves into the concept of Earth as a 'learning ground' for starseeds, exploring how they experience specific challenges to fulfill karmic obligations or learn important lessons.

Earth as a Learning Ground

Starseeds often consider their time on Earth as an opportunity for growth and learning, akin to a student enrolled in a complex, multifaceted school. In this 'Earth school,' each life event, relationship, and challenge can be viewed as a class or course designed to teach specific lessons. These lessons may range from learning compassion and empathy to understanding the complexities of free will and destiny.

Just as in a regular school, failure to grasp a lesson usually means repetition. This is often what people mean when they talk about 'karmic cycles.' Starseeds, with their heightened sensitivity to cosmic energies, may find themselves especially conscious of these repeating patterns. Breaking free from such cycles often involves a deep inner reckoning, an epiphany that enables the starseed to integrate the lesson and thus, move forward.

Karmic Obligations and Agreements

Another important concept that comes into play is that of karma. In Eastern philosophies, karma is the law of cause and effect; every action has a consequence, and this consequence could carry over into future lifetimes. Starseeds often believe in the existence of karmic contracts or agreements that they've made before incarnating on Earth. These contracts outline the key relationships and situations they will encounter in life, serving as a sort of syllabus for their Earthly mission.

It is not uncommon for starseeds to feel a strong sense of purpose or obligation towards certain individuals or challenges. This is often indicative of a karmic tie, something that needs to be addressed and possibly resolved. The nature of these obligations can vary significantly, from nurturing a soul connection to resolving conflicts that have persisted across lifetimes.

Navigating Earthly Challenges

Starseeds are not exempt from the struggles that accompany earthly life. In fact, they may face unique challenges tailored to prompt growth and wisdom. Earthly difficulties, whether in relationships, careers, or personal development, often serve as the practical exams of this cosmic school. The objective isn't merely to 'pass' these tests but to understand their underlying lessons.

Some starseeds find that they attract the same types of challenges repeatedly until they confront the root issue. This repetition is not meant to be a punishment but rather an indicator that a certain lesson has not yet been absorbed. The key to breaking this loop is often found in self-awareness, emotional intelligence, and spiritual maturity.

The Role of Free Will

While it may sound like everything is predestined, the principle of free will remains crucial in the starseed experience. Think of it this way: If Earth is a school, then karmic agreements and challenges are the curriculum. However, how one engages with that curriculum is entirely up to the individual.

Starseeds, like anyone else, have the freedom to make choices. These choices can either align them further with their earthly missions and cosmic origins or steer them off course. In either scenario, the free will decisions they make also contribute to their learning experience, adding nuances and complexities to their Earthly tenure.

Spiritual Growth and Ascension

As starseeds navigate their karmic lessons and life challenges, they also contribute to their spiritual development and, by extension, the collective spiritual evolution. The insights gained, wisdom gathered, and karma resolved not only serve the individual starseed but also resonate at a frequency that benefits humanity and Earth as a whole. It's as if each starseed, by passing their personal' classes,' helps the collective grade point average of the planet.

In summary, the Earthly experience offers a rich tapestry of lessons and karmic interactions that are particularly poignant for starseeds. By considering Earth as a school, starseeds can better understand the significance of their life events, relationships, and challenges. Whether it's through fulfilling karmic obligations, breaking free from repetitive cycles, or making conscious choices, each experience provides invaluable lessons. These lessons not only propel individual starseeds on their spiritual journey but also contribute to the broader cosmic mission of elevating collective consciousness.

CHAPTER 9: INTERSTELLAR COMMUNICATION: CONNECTING WITH STAR FAMILIES

The journey of a starseed is often marked by a yearning for connection, not just with the earthly realm but also with their celestial origins. This chapter explores the different avenues through which starseeds can forge a deeper connection with their star families, which are believed to be entities or consciousnesses from the same star system as the starseed. We'll delve into the most commonly cited methods such as meditation, dreams, and psychic experiences, to shed light on how starseeds can tune into the frequencies of their galactic kin.

Meditation as a Cosmic Bridge

It has been known for a very long time that meditation is an extremely effective method for both personal development and spiritual advancement. In the context of starseeds, meditation has the potential to function as a connection to their star families. While there are various meditation techniques, the emphasis here is on focused intention and visualization. Starseeds often use guided meditations that take them through celestial journeys to meet their star families. Some claim to have experienced astral travel or out-of-body experiences during such meditative states, providing a tangible feeling of having visited their home star systems.

Dreams and Lucid Dreaming

The realm of dreams is another sphere where starseeds report connections with their star families. Unlike the waking state, the dream state is believed to have less rigid boundaries between dimensions, allowing easier interaction with higher-frequency entities. A particularly potent form of dreaming is known as lucid dreaming, which occurs when the dreamer is conscious that they are dreaming. Starseeds have the ability to lucidly inquire to meet their star families or travel to their native star systems while they are experiencing the state of lucid dreaming. These dream encounters often leave an indelible impact, imparting wisdom, guidance, and sometimes even specific missions.

Psychic Experiences and Clairvoyance

Beyond meditation and dreams, some starseeds report psychic experiences as a means of connecting with their star families. Clairvoyance, or clear-seeing, is commonly cited. This involves receiving visions or images, either spontaneously or through focused practices like scrying. Another form is clairaudience, or clear-hearing, where starseeds receive auditory messages from their galactic kin. These psychic experiences can happen randomly or may be invoked through intentional spiritual practices.

Signs and Synchronicities

Not all connections with star families are as dramatic as astral travel or clairvoyant visions. Sometimes, the communication is subtle and comes through signs and synchronicities. For instance, starseeds often report seeing specific number sequences, like 11:11 or 444, as a form of message from their star families. Nature signs such as unique cloud formations, the sudden appearance of certain animals, or even meteorological phenomena like rainbows are also viewed as meaningful.

Channeling and Mediumship

Some starseeds, particularly those with advanced psychic abilities, turn to channeling as a means to connect with their star families. Channeling involves entering a meditative state and allowing a higher-dimensional entity to speak through you. While this is a more advanced practice requiring careful discernment and preparation, many find it to be a direct and profound way to receive guidance and wisdom from their galactic kin.

Summary

The search for connection is a fundamental aspect of the human experience, and for starseeds, this extends to their cosmic families. Through various methods like meditation, dreams, psychic experiences, signs, and channeling, starseeds seek to communicate with their celestial counterparts. Each of these methods offers its unique set of experiences and benefits, but all aim to help starseeds gain insights, guidance, and a sense of belonging as they navigate their earthly missions. Whether subtle or profound, these connections serve to remind starseeds of their galactic heritage, guiding them as they fulfill their roles in Earth's evolutionary trajectory.

CHAPTER 10: STARSEEDS AND ASCENSION: THE JOURNEY TO 5D

The notion of Earth ascending to a fifth-dimensional reality (often termed "5D") is a theme deeply intertwined with the starseed narrative. This chapter aims to explore this fascinating and somewhat enigmatic subject, focusing particularly on the role that starseeds play in this transformative process. We'll delve into the concept of vibrational frequencies, the idea of multidimensionality, and how starseeds act as catalysts for this planetary shift.

Understanding Fifth-Dimensional Reality

Before we can discuss the starseeds' role in the ascension, it's important to grasp what is meant by "fifth-dimensional reality." In contrast to the three spatial dimensions and one time dimension that we are accustomed to, it is hypothesized that the fifth dimension, also known as 5D, is a higher vibrating state in which interactions are governed by unconditional love, compassion, and universal understanding. This state is not so much a 'place' but rather a frequency, a mode of perception and experience that transcends our traditional senses.

Vibrational Frequencies and Multidimensionality

Everything in the universe, at its most fundamental level, is composed of energy vibrating at various frequencies. Even solid matter is energy, tightly packed and vibrating at a slower rate. Dimensions are often considered different levels of frequency, and moving from one to another involves a shift in vibration.

The concept of multidimensionality suggests that various dimensions exist concurrently, but are generally imperceptible to us because our senses are tuned to the third-dimensional frequency. However, starseeds and other spiritually awakened individuals often report experiences that suggest they have tapped into these higher dimensions—either momentarily or for longer periods.

The Role of Starseeds in Ascension

Many believe that starseeds serve as energetic anchors during Earth's ascension process. Due to their cosmic origins and unique vibrational signatures, starseeds are thought to be naturally aligned with higher-dimensional frequencies. Their role, therefore, is twofold. First, they act as facilitators for others, helping to elevate collective human consciousness. Second, they serve as conduits for higher-dimensional energies to filter into Earth's energetic grid.

Starseeds often find themselves drawn to spiritual practices, energy work, and other modalities that facilitate the flow of higher-vibrational energies. This isn't coincidental but rather an integral part of their earthly mission. By embracing these roles, starseeds help to shift the collective consciousness toward a 5D reality.

Challenges and Responsibilities

Although their mission may be divinely orchestrated, starseeds also encounter numerous challenges in their journey. The dense, lower-vibrational energies prevalent in our current reality can be draining and even disorienting for them. Many feel the strain of living between two worlds: the higher-dimensional realms they originated from and the third-dimensional Earth they have come to assist.

Moreover, the responsibility of acting as an anchor for higher frequencies should not be taken lightly. Consistency in spiritual practice, self-care, and maintaining energetic hygiene are crucial for starseeds to effectively fulfill their roles in the ascension process.

Synchronicities and Ascension Symptoms

Many starseeds report experiencing heightened synchronicities and so-called "ascension symptoms" as they align more closely with 5D frequencies. These may include changes in sleep patterns, heightened sensitivity to energies, and even temporary physical discomforts like headaches or body aches. These symptoms are considered by some as signs of DNA activation or energetic recalibration and usually subside as one acclimates to the higher frequencies.

Summary

The idea of Earth's transition into a fifth-dimensional reality is integral to the starseed narrative. In this chapter, we explored how starseeds serve as energetic facilitators and conduits in this planetary shift. As naturally attuned beings to higher frequencies, they play a critical role in raising collective human consciousness and anchoring higher-dimensional energies. Yet, the journey is far from smooth, laden with both challenges and responsibilities. By remaining committed to their spiritual practices and their mission, starseeds stand as vital players in the evolutionary leap toward a fifth-dimensional Earth.

CHAPTER 11: TWIN FLAMES AND SOUL GROUPS: GALACTIC RELATIONSHIPS

The realm of starseeds is not just limited to their individual journeys or missions on Earth; it also encompasses the deeper, more intricate web of relationships they share with other souls. These connections, often termed as twin flames and soul groups, hold particular significance in the life of a starseed. Understanding these relationships can offer profound insights into the emotional, spiritual, and even cosmic dimensions of a starseed's existence. In this chapter, we'll delve into the significance of these galactic relationships and explore how they influence both earthly and cosmic experiences.

Twin Flames: The Mirror Soul

The concept of twin flames refers to two souls that originate from the same source but take different incarnational journeys. These souls are said to have the same energetic signature or frequency and to have a connection with one another. In the context of starseeds, the idea of twin flames extends into the cosmic realm, where these souls are believed to have incarnated from the same star system or even the same soul family. The relationship between twin flames transcends earthly definitions of love or partnership; it is often characterized by a sense of completeness and unconditional love, accompanied by a mission or purpose that the two are meant to fulfill together.

Contrary to popular misconceptions, the meeting of twin flames is not always smooth or free from challenges. The relationship is often likened to a 'mirror,' revealing to each individual their deepest fears, insecurities, and potential for growth. While the presence of a twin flame can bring about intense joy and spiritual awakening, it can also trigger significant life changes, acting as a catalyst for personal and spiritual evolution.

Soul Groups: The Galactic Family

While twin flames are often considered a pair of souls closely bonded together, soul groups consist of a larger number of souls who share a common mission, frequency, or origin. Think of a soul group as a galactic family where each member holds a specific role or function aimed at fulfilling a collective mission. For starseeds, their soul group often comprises other starseeds from the same star system, and they may incarnate together to work on joint missions, such as environmental healing or social change.

Being part of a soul group provides a support system that aids in the realization of individual and collective missions. Members of a soul group often incarnate together in different lifetimes, across various dimensions, and sometimes even in other planetary systems. Recognizing your soul group can provide comfort, guidance, and a deeper sense of belonging, both on Earth and in cosmic terms.

Earthly Interactions and Relationships

Starseeds may find that their earthly relationships are deeply influenced by their connections with twin flames and soul groups. These relationships often act as a 'magnet,' pulling the starseeds toward significant life experiences, karmic lessons, or mission-oriented activities. The recognition of a twin flame or a soul group member often happens through synchronous events, vivid dreams, or intuitive insights, and the meeting itself can be a significant milestone in the starseed's awakening process.

The Cosmic Significance

From a cosmic perspective, the relationships between twin flames and soul groups are not mere emotional or interpersonal bonds; they serve a higher purpose in the grand scheme of universal evolution. Twin flames often hold a synergistic energy that, when combined, can be channeled into fulfilling missions that are integral to Earth's ascension or even the higher evolutionary trajectory of the cosmos. Similarly, soul groups function like nodes in a cosmic network, facilitating the flow of energy and information that is crucial for the development of consciousness across dimensions.

The Balancing Act

While it's essential to understand the gravity of these relationships, it's equally crucial not to become so engrossed in seeking or nurturing these connections that one loses sight of individual missions or earthly responsibilities. Balance is key. Even within these deeply spiritual relationships, there is room for individual growth, free will, and the human experiences that contribute to soul evolution.

In summary, the realm of twin flames and soul groups adds a complex yet enriching layer to the starseed experience. These relationships go beyond mere earthly interactions, offering a glimpse into the intricate web of cosmic connections. They not only contribute to individual awakening and mission fulfillment but also play a significant role in the evolutionary schemes of the universe. Understanding and honoring these connections can lead to a more harmonious, fulfilling, and purposeful life, both on Earth and in the greater cosmic landscape.

CHAPTER 12: NAVIGATING EARTHLY CHALLENGES: STARSEED STRUGGLES

While the concept of being a starseed can sound enchanting, filled with cosmic purposes and divine missions, it's crucial to acknowledge that this path is not without its challenges. Whether you identify as a starseed or are keenly interested in understanding their experience, it's important to explore the unique struggles that these individuals face in aligning their cosmic objectives with earthly realities.

The Identity Crisis

Many starseeds experience what could best be described as an "identity crisis." Their awakening may lead them to profound existential questions that are difficult to grapple with. Who am I? Where do I really come from? What am I supposed to do here? These queries can lead to a sense of isolation, as starseeds often feel like they don't quite fit in, neither fully belonging to their earthly environment nor having a clear connection to their galactic origins.

The Struggle with Mundane Reality

Starseeds often feel a sense of disconnection with the societal norms and structures that dictate the course of everyday life on Earth. Tasks like holding down a 9-to-5 job, managing finances, or even maintaining traditional relationships can seem draining and somewhat trivial compared to their perceived cosmic mission. This struggle with the mundane aspects of earthly life can lead to stress, anxiety, and, at times, disillusionment.

Social and Emotional Challenges

The experience of feeling like an outsider isn't merely philosophical for starseeds; it can have real emotional and social consequences. While starseeds are often empathic and sensitive, making them great listeners and friends, their unconventional outlooks can sometimes make it difficult for them to relate to others. The sense of 'otherness' can lead to periods of loneliness and could even affect mental health if not managed effectively.

Divergence in Spiritual and Material Goals

Another common struggle lies in aligning their higher spiritual aspirations with the practical demands of earthly life. For instance, while a starseed might feel a calling to engage in humanitarian work, the financial and practical limitations can seem insurmountable. Balancing the spiritual and the material is a significant challenge, often requiring starseeds to make compromises that can feel deeply unsettling.

Misunderstanding and Skepticism from Society

Lastly, the starseed experience is not universally accepted or understood by mainstream culture. Skepticism abounds, and this lack of acceptance can make starseeds feel marginalized or misunderstood, impacting their self-esteem and confidence in fulfilling their mission.

Navigational Tools for Earthly Challenges

So, how do starseeds navigate these earthly challenges? A key aspect is grounding, which helps in balancing their ethereal, cosmic aspects with the tangible, earthly realm. Practices such as meditation, nature walks, and even engaging in creative pursuits like art and music can offer this grounding effect. Some starseeds also find solace in like-minded communities, both online and offline, that provide the emotional and intellectual support needed to navigate these challenges. Counseling and therapeutic techniques, particularly those that are holistic and incorporate spiritual dimensions, can also be effective.

In summary, the path of a starseed is not without its struggles, particularly when it comes to aligning their celestial missions with terrestrial challenges. From facing identity crises and feeling disconnected from societal norms to dealing with the complexities of emotional well-being, these individuals often have to traverse a winding and often lonely road. However, by adopting practices that provide grounding and emotional balance, and by seeking support from understanding communities, starseeds can find their way through these challenges, serving as beacons of light in both earthly and cosmic dimensions.

CHAPTER 13: TOOLS AND CRYSTALS: AMPLIFYING STARSEED ENERGIES

For the Starseed, navigating the Earth plane can sometimes feel like wading through an unfamiliar landscape. Given their unique cosmic heritage and earthly missions, it's no surprise that many Starseeds are drawn to various tools and crystals that can assist them in amplifying their energies and fulfilling their roles. In this chapter, we'll delve into some of the most cherished tools and crystals within the Starseed community, exploring how these aids can complement their vibrational frequencies and assist them in their cosmic quests.

The Resonance of Crystals

One of the most popular ways Starseeds can heighten their energies is through the use of crystals. These Earth-grown minerals are not only beautiful to look at but also come with their own sets of frequencies and properties. For example, Amethyst, often recognized for its striking purple hue, is commonly associated with spiritual growth and protection. It's a favored choice for opening the third-eye chakra, which is integral for intuition and spiritual insight.

On the other hand, Rose Quartz, known for its soft pink color, is linked with heart-centered energies like love and compassion—qualities that many Starseeds naturally resonate with. It's believed that holding or wearing Rose Quartz can enhance one's ability to give and receive love, both from others and oneself. For Starseeds who often feel like outsiders on this planet, the comforting frequencies of Rose Quartz can serve as a gentle reminder that love is a universal language.

The Role of Sacred Geometry

Sacred geometry refers to the patterns and shapes that are considered to have spiritual significance, including circles, spirals, and the Flower of Life design. Starseeds often incorporate these shapes into their meditation practices or even wear them as jewelry. The Merkaba, a 3D interlocking triangles shape, is particularly significant for many Starseeds. It is often employed in spiritual practices to aid in achieving higher states of consciousness and can be visualized during meditation to assist in astral travel or connecting with higher-dimensional beings.

Sound and Frequency Tools

Sound healing has been an integral part of various cultures for centuries, and Starseeds are no exception to its allure. From tuning forks to singing bowls, the application of sound frequencies can have a profound effect on our energetic bodies. Tibetan singing bowls, for instance, have been used in meditation and healing rituals and are thought to balance the chakras and calm the mind. The sound frequency emitted by these bowls resonates with the body's natural frequency, facilitating alignment and balance, two attributes that are often essential for Starseeds in carrying out their earthly missions.

Divining Tools: Pendulums and Oracle Cards

Starseeds often seek guidance and confirmation for their path, and tools like pendulums and oracle cards can be quite useful in this regard. A pendulum, usually a weighted object suspended from a string, can provide yes-or-no answers to questions based on its movements. It serves as an extension of the user's intuition. Oracle cards, on the other hand, offer more nuanced messages and are often employed to provide insights into specific life situations or challenges.

The Power of Intention

In utilizing these tools and crystals, it's crucial to remember that intention plays a significant role. The efficacy of any tool—be it a crystal or a piece of sacred geometry—is amplified by the intention one sets while using it. Before employing any of these tools, it may be helpful to center oneself through meditation, and clearly articulate the aim or question at hand. This makes for a more potent energetic interaction, aligning the tool's inherent properties with the individual's unique vibrational signature.

Summary

Starseeds have a variety of tools and crystals at their disposal for enhancing their energies and aiding in their earthly and cosmic missions. From the vibrational qualities of specific crystals like Amethyst and Rose Quartz to the intricate designs of sacred geometry and the frequencies of sound healing instruments, these tools can serve as invaluable companions. However, the power of intention cannot be overlooked; it acts as the keystone that bridges the user with the tool, magnifying its effects. Whether you identify as a Starseed or are simply interested in the metaphysical properties of these tools, incorporating them into your spiritual practice could serve as a valuable enhancement in your journey toward higher consciousness.

CHAPTER 14: STARSEEDS IN THE NEW AGE: MODERN ROLES AND ACTIVATIONS

As we navigate the complexities of our modern world, it becomes increasingly clear that we are in a time of great transformation. Social paradigms are shifting, environmental challenges are escalating, and old structures are breaking down to make way for new perspectives. In this context, the role of starseeds—souls believed to have cosmic origins with a specific mission on Earth—becomes even more intriguing. In this chapter, we will explore how starseeds fit into the tapestry of contemporary life, particularly focusing on their evolving roles within spiritual communities and socio-environmental causes.

Spiritual Communities: Beacons of Light and Wisdom

One of the most visible platforms where starseeds are making their presence felt is within spiritual communities. These communities serve as collective spaces that foster a sense of unity, explore higher dimensions of reality, and promote individual as well as collective enlightenment. Starseeds often find themselves naturally drawn to such gatherings, where their inherent spiritual attributes can shine most brightly.

In these settings, starseeds frequently assume roles that range from teachers and mentors to energy healers and intuitive guides. With their ability to tap into cosmic wisdom and share insights on ascension, vibrational frequencies, and multidimensional living, they serve as invaluable contributors to spiritual dialogues and practices. Their presence often functions as a catalyst for deeper awareness and awakening among community members, enabling transformative experiences that resonate far beyond the individual level.

Socio-Environmental Activism: Guardians of Earth

Starseeds are not only concerned with metaphysical or spiritual matters; many are actively involved in social and environmental causes, deeply committed to making a tangible difference on Earth. Given their cosmic perspective, they recognize the interconnectedness of all life and feel a strong obligation to protect and nurture our planet.

Whether it's through campaigning against environmental degradation, advocating for social justice, or participating in community-based initiatives, starseeds bring a unique set of skills and perspectives to the table. Their ability to view issues from a higher vantage point allows them to approach problems holistically, often suggesting solutions that are innovative and sustainable. For instance, they might advocate for permaculture as a way to heal the Earth or promote alternative economic models that prioritize collective well-being over individual profit.

Online Platforms: Spreading Cosmic Awareness

The digital age has enabled starseeds to connect with like-minded individuals across the globe, giving them an unprecedented platform to share their wisdom and fulfill their earthly missions. Social media, podcasts, blogs, and other online channels have become popular avenues for starseeds to disseminate their messages, offering guidance, and providing support to those who are in the process of awakening.

This expansive reach has also led to what some refer to as "activations," moments or experiences often facilitated by starseeds that trigger profound personal and spiritual transformations in others. Through guided meditations, energy healings, or simply sharing enlightening content, starseeds utilize the power of the internet to activate latent potentials in individuals, thereby accelerating their journey toward higher consciousness.

The Power of Community: Collective Activations

It's important to recognize that the impact of starseeds is amplified when they work collectively. Groups of starseeds often come together for specific purposes—whether it's organizing mass meditations to raise the planet's vibrational frequency or collaborating on social projects aimed at enhancing community well-being. When aligned in intention, their collective energy can set the stage for significant shifts in consciousness and tangible improvements in earthly conditions.

These "collective activations" go beyond individual pursuits and tap into the power of unity, often producing results that are both deeply transformative and far-reaching. They embody the principle that the whole is greater than the sum of its parts, proving that when united in purpose, starseeds can be a formidable force for positive change.

Conclusion

As we continue to traverse the multifaceted landscape of modern existence, the roles of starseeds are becoming increasingly relevant and expansive. They serve as beacons of light in spiritual communities, champions for socio-environmental causes, and connectors in the digital realm, guiding individuals and collectives toward a more conscious and harmonious existence. By working both individually and collectively, they are not only fulfilling their unique missions but also contributing to a larger narrative of global transformation. Indeed, the starseeds, with their cosmic wisdom and earthly commitments, are playing a vital role in shaping the New Age, helping humanity align with higher frequencies and prepare for the next phase of its evolutionary journey.

CHAPTER 15: TOWARD THE FUTURE: STARSEEDS IN THE COSMIC EVOLUTION

The notion of starseeds—souls with extraterrestrial origins—has captivated minds and imaginations, leading to much discussion and speculation. What seems clear is that the purpose of starseeds extends beyond individual missions or earthly roles. Rather, they are envisioned as part of a collective endeavor, contributing to a grander plan in the cosmic evolution of consciousness. This chapter explores the long-term implications of starseed incarnations and what they might mean for the unfolding narrative of consciousness, both earthly and cosmic.

The Web of Consciousness

At the heart of starseed philosophy lies a concept not dissimilar to certain Eastern spiritual traditions: the interconnectedness of all life forms. This web of consciousness is viewed as spanning not just across Earth but across the universe. Starseeds, with their multidimensional origins, are often seen as connectors, linking different dimensions of reality and facilitating the flow of cosmic consciousness into earthly realms. This concept aligns with quantum theories that propose the interconnectedness of all things at a fundamental level.

Planetary Ascension and Its Cosmic Repercussions

Starseeds are often described as catalysts for change, especially concerning Earth's ascension to a higher vibrational state, commonly referred to as the 5th dimension. The belief is that Earth's ascension has implications beyond its terrestrial boundaries, impacting neighboring planets and possibly entire star systems. Some spiritual philosophies propose that the Earth is like a "library" of experiences and learnings for the cosmos, and as the Earth ascends, so does the wisdom it contributes to the universal repository.

Collective Karma and Universal Balance

The concept of karma, often limited to individual actions and repercussions, extends to a collective level in starseed ideology. The actions of a planet, or even a galaxy, can create ripples across the fabric of cosmic consciousness. Starseeds are seen as facilitators in balancing collective karma by incarnating in crucial times and places, contributing to planetary healing, and raising the vibration of collective human consciousness.

Evolutionary Cycles and Cosmic Seasons

Just like Earth has its seasons and cycles, spiritual cosmology posits that the cosmos too goes through vast cycles of evolution and change. These are sometimes called "Yugas" in Hinduism or "World Ages" in various mythologies. Starseeds are thought to incarnate in significant cosmic "seasons," aligning their missions with the needs of the time. For instance, their increased presence on Earth now might indicate we're at a significant juncture in a cosmic cycle, a time of potential transformation or renewal.

The Future: A Symphony of Souls

Starseeds, Earth souls, and other cosmic entities could be envisioned as notes in a grand cosmic symphony. Each plays its part, contributes its tone, and the resultant music is the ever-evolving state of cosmic consciousness. The future, from this viewpoint, is not linear but a complex interplay of multitudes of souls from various dimensions, each contributing to a grander narrative of cosmic evolution.

In the long-term perspective, the role of starseeds is profound yet humble. It suggests that each of us, whether starseed or Earth soul, plays a part in the cosmic tapestry of life. In this orchestra of existence, each instrument has its unique note to play. But when played together, in harmony, they can create a celestial music that resounds through the very core of the cosmos.

The discussion of starseeds' involvement in cosmic evolution weaves together threads from quantum physics, ancient spiritual traditions, and modern metaphysical concepts. It paints a picture of a universe rich in interconnectedness and purpose, where the actions of individual souls can reverberate through the cosmos. While these ideas might stretch the bounds of conventional thinking, they offer a vision of a deeply interconnected universe, full of potential for co-creative evolution. And in that expansive view, the role of starseeds becomes a fascinating subject not only for individual quests for self-understanding but also for pondering the complex and wondrous dynamics of cosmic evolution.

CHAPTER 16: CHAKRAS AND ENERGY CENTERS: STARSEED ANATOMY

Understanding the energetic anatomy of starseeds requires diving deep into the concept of chakras and other subtle energy centers. While chakras are often discussed in the context of mainstream spirituality, yoga, and healing arts, they hold specific significance for starseeds. The particular arrangement, activation, and function of these energy centers may differ somewhat for starseeds, emphasizing their unique cosmic roles and origin.

The Traditional Chakra System

For context, let's first briefly review the traditional chakra system as understood in ancient Hindu and Buddhist philosophies. The chakra system is made up of seven primary energy centers that are arranged in a line down the spinal column. There are unique psychological activities, physical organs, and endocrine glands that are connected to each chakra. These are known as the Root, Sacral, Heart, Throat, Third Eye, and Crown chakras, and they are located in ascending order from the base of the spine to the top of the head. Through practices like meditation, Reiki, and Kundalini Yoga, individuals aim to awaken and balance these chakras for better physical and spiritual well-being.

Starseed-Specific Chakras

Now, when we consider starseeds, some anecdotal accounts and channeled information suggest the presence of additional chakras outside the physical body. These additional chakras are often described as 'transpersonal' or 'cosmic' chakras and are believed to connect starseeds directly to higher dimensions, their star families, and their galactic origins. Some commonly discussed ones are the Earth Star chakra (below the feet), the Soul Star chakra (above the head), and even the Stellar Gateway chakra, which is considered to be a link to the divine or the cosmos itself.

Understanding these additional chakras could be key for starseeds to anchor higher-dimensional energies into the Earth plane and to fulfill their unique missions. Practices like advanced meditation, shamanic journeying, and high-frequency energy work are sometimes recommended to activate these chakras.

Energetic Layers and Auric Fields

Beyond chakras, starseeds are often said to possess intricate auric fields that might be more sensitive or expansive than those of average individuals. The auric field, commonly divided into seven layers, serves as an energetic shield and communication system between the individual and the external world. For starseeds, each layer could be highly responsive to cosmic energies, enabling them to be naturally intuitive, empathic, or even psychic.

Energy Sensitivity and Protection

Because of their unique energetic anatomy, starseeds may often find themselves sensitive to the energies around them—both positive and negative. This makes the practice of energetic protection crucial. Techniques such as grounding, shielding, and regular cleansing of the auric field can be particularly effective. Crystals like black tourmaline or smoky quartz are often recommended for grounding, while visualizations of protective light can serve as energetic shields.

Role in Ascension and Earthly Missions

Understanding and aligning one's chakras and energy centers is not only a personal endeavor for starseeds but also ties back to their broader cosmic missions. The more balanced and activated their energy system, the more effective they are in channeling higher frequencies and wisdom down to Earth. This is considered vital in assisting the planet through its ongoing ascension process, making it possible for humanity to resonate with higher dimensions of consciousness more readily.

In summary, the unique energetic anatomy of starseeds includes not only the traditional seven-chakra system but also additional cosmic chakras, sensitive auric fields, and specialized sensitivities to energy. Acknowledging and working with these unique attributes can not only aid starseeds in their personal spiritual journeys but also better equip them to fulfill their earthly missions. Practices for energy activation and protection can serve as vital tools for starseeds as they navigate both their earthly lives and cosmic responsibilities.

CHAPTER 17: DIVINATION AND SIGNS: GUIDANCE FOR STARSEEDS

Divination is an ancient practice that has been used for centuries to seek guidance, gain insight, and connect with higher powers. For starseeds—souls with cosmic origins—divination tools like tarot cards, astrology, and numerology offer a unique window into their Earthly missions and galactic journeys. Let's delve into how these age-old systems can provide practical and spiritual guidance for starseeds.

Tarot and Oracle Cards: Symbolic Guidance

There are 78 cards in a deck of tarot cards, and each one has an image on it that represents something. Tarot cards are used for divination. Oracle cards, on the other hand, vary in number and themes. Both are intuitive tools that starseeds can use to gain insights into their daily lives and long-term missions. When pulling cards, starseeds might find that certain cards resonate with them more powerfully than others, perhaps pointing to a past life experience or a celestial influence.

What's noteworthy is that the Tarot isn't just about foretelling the future. Its archetypes can serve as reflections of a starseed's inner world and mission. Cards like "The Star" and "The World" often resonate deeply with starseeds, pointing to their otherworldly origins and the universal scale of their aspirations.

Astrology: Navigating Celestial Influences

Astrology, the study of celestial bodies' movements and their influence on human affairs, holds a special allure for starseeds. Considering their cosmic roots, it seems natural for starseeds to feel a strong connection to astrology. Many believe that their astrological charts can reveal not just their Earthly tendencies, but also their galactic predispositions. In particular, the placements of celestial bodies like Uranus, Neptune, and Pluto are often looked at for hints of a starseed's cosmic lineage and mission.

Certain astrological configurations, such as having a significant number of planets in 'water signs,' might indicate a starseed's propensity for emotional sensitivity and spiritual work. It's often recommended that starseeds consult professional astrologers who can tailor their interpretations to fit the unique cosmic complexities that starseeds present.

Numerology: The Language of Numbers

Numerology, the study of the mystical meanings of numbers and their influence on human life, offers another avenue for starseeds to gain insights. In numerology, each number has a unique vibrational essence and symbolism. For starseeds, numbers can serve as signposts on their earthly journey, pointing them toward their higher purpose or reminding them of their celestial origins.

Life Path Numbers, calculated from one's birthdate, can provide significant insights into one's purpose and challenges in this lifetime. Similarly, Soul Urge Numbers, derived from the vowels in one's name, can shed light on inner desires and unconscious drives. Observing repeating numbers or numerical patterns, often referred to as 'angel numbers,' can also serve as affirmations or messages from their star families or spirit guides.

Runes and I Ching: Ancient Wisdom

Runes, characters from ancient alphabets particularly used by the Germanic peoples, and the I Ching, an ancient Chinese divination text, are other tools that starseeds can explore. Both offer profound wisdom and guidance, although they originate from distinct cultural and spiritual traditions.

Runes are often cast in a similar manner to tarot cards and can provide insights into specific questions or general life circumstances. The I Ching involves tossing a set of coins to produce a hexagram, which is then interpreted through poetic and philosophical text. For starseeds interested in connecting with earthly ancient wisdom while considering their cosmic origins, these forms of divination can be especially enriching.

Ethical Considerations and Responsible Use

As starseeds engage with these divinatory practices, it's essential to approach them responsibly and ethically. While these tools can offer guidance, they should not replace one's own intuition or rational decision-making processes. It's also crucial to respect the cultural origins of these practices, especially when they come from traditions outside one's own heritage.

In summary, divinatory practices offer a rich tapestry of wisdom and guidance that starseeds can weave into their lives. Whether through the intricate symbolism of tarot cards, the celestial mapping of astrology, the mathematical mystique of numerology, or the ancient wisdom of runes and the I Ching, starseeds have a plethora of tools to gain insights into their earthly missions and cosmic origins. These practices can help starseeds navigate the complexities of being terrestrial beings with celestial souls, and serve as invaluable aids on their journey towards fulfilling their higher purpose.

CHAPTER 18: STARSEEDS AND ECOLOGY: GUARDIANS OF THE EARTH

In the context of spiritual and cosmic diversity, starseeds often find themselves at the intersection of the metaphysical and the tangible. One realm where this union is particularly compelling is in the area of environmental conservation. Starseeds are often deeply connected to the Earth, not just as a host planet but as a living entity that requires care and guardianship. This chapter delves into the symbiotic relationship between starseeds and ecology, exploring how their cosmic mission frequently aligns with the principles of environmental activism and sustainability.

The Cosmic Connection to Earth

Starseeds are generally considered to come from advanced civilizations where the understanding of ecological balance and sustainability may be more profound than what is currently understood on Earth. Consequently, when incarnating here, many starseeds find themselves inexplicably drawn to environmental causes. They may feel a visceral connection to the planet's ecosystems, be they forests, oceans, or mountains. This is more than just a predilection; it's often seen as a component of their broader mission to elevate planetary consciousness.

Whether or not one subscribes to the spiritual notion of Gaia Theory—the Earth as a single, self-regulating organism—it's undeniable that starseeds often perceive Earth in a way that resonates with this concept. They may see the planet as a living entity, deserving of respect and care, as any sentient being would be.

Eco-Spirituality and Starseeds

Within various spiritual traditions, there exists the idea of eco-spirituality, a blend of spiritual faith and ecological activism. In this arena, starseeds often find a natural home. Their intuitive wisdom from other realms or lifetimes can be a potent force for innovative solutions to environmental problems. Whether it's advocating for renewable energy sources, participating in tree-planting initiatives, or joining forces with local conservation efforts, the starseed's approach to ecology is often holistic, seeing the interconnections between all forms of life.

Eco-spirituality isn't solely about combating climate change or protecting endangered species—important as those issues are. It also emphasizes the spiritual enrichment that comes from a harmonious relationship with the Earth. Starseeds, with their inherent drive towards unity and higher consciousness, often find this spiritual aspect of ecology to be an essential part of their earthly mission.

Earth Healing Rituals and Practices

Starseeds frequently employ metaphysical techniques for Earth healing, contributing to the planet's well-being on both physical and energetic levels. Practices such as Earth grid work—where individuals visualize or physically mark out sacred geometrical patterns on the Earth—are one such method. Additionally, techniques like crystal healing and shamanic journeys may also be used to communicate with the Earth's spirit or to heal damaged lands.

It is not uncommon for starseeds to gather in groups for synchronized meditations focused on Earth healing, sometimes even timing these gatherings to coincide with significant cosmic events like solstices or planetary alignments. The underlying belief here is that collective intention magnifies the healing potential, making these practices more potent.

The Interconnected Web of Life

Starseeds often feel a sense of urgency about ecological matters, grounded in the understanding that all life is interconnected. From an earthly perspective, this means recognizing the links between human activities, environmental degradation, and social justice issues. From a cosmic viewpoint, it encompasses the idea that Earth's well-being is part of a larger galactic equilibrium.

Therefore, for many starseeds, environmental activism is a dual endeavor. On one hand, it serves the immediate, pressing needs of the Earth; on the other, it contributes to the planet's vibrational frequency, which is thought to have cascading effects throughout the cosmos. Such activism might involve grassroots organization, policy advocacy, or even pioneering new technologies that are in harmony with the Earth.

Summary

In summary, the intersection of starseeds and ecology is a multifaceted relationship that combines spiritual beliefs, cosmic wisdom, and hands-on activism. Starseeds often view their commitment to Earth's well-being as a manifestation of their broader cosmic missions, a calling that aligns closely with the principles of environmental conservation and sustainability. Through various avenues, ranging from eco-spirituality to Earth healing rituals and advocacy, starseeds contribute to both the physical and energetic healing of the planet. Their actions not only serve the immediate ecological needs but also resonate on a cosmic scale, acknowledging the intricate web of life that connects us all.

CHAPTER 19: ACTIVATING DNA: THE SCIENCE BEHIND STARSEEDS

In the realm of starseeds and their unique missions on Earth, a term often discussed is "DNA activation." This chapter delves into what DNA activation implies in the context of starseeds and examines whether there is any scientific basis for such claims. Though the concept of DNA activation has esoteric underpinnings, it intersects with genetics, epigenetics, and even quantum physics.

The Concept of DNA Activation in Spiritual Discourse

In spiritual communities, DNA activation is often described as the awakening of dormant strands of DNA that supposedly grant an individual enhanced abilities, higher levels of consciousness, or a deeper understanding of their cosmic origins. According to proponents of this idea, humans possess more than just the standard two strands of DNA, with the additional strands remaining "inactive" or "dormant" until an awakening process occurs. This activation is said to allow starseeds, in particular, to tap into their innate spiritual gifts and cosmic wisdom.

The Scientific Understanding of DNA

To evaluate these claims, it's essential to understand what DNA is from a scientific standpoint. Deoxyribonucleic acid (DNA) serves as the hereditary material in humans and nearly all other organisms. DNA is composed of two strands that coil around each other to form a double helix. Genes, the functional units of heredity, are segments of DNA that code for specific proteins, ultimately controlling an organism's characteristics and functions.

Current scientific understanding recognizes only two active strands of DNA in humans, and there's no empirical evidence to support the existence of additional "inactive" strands. Genome mapping and sequencing projects like the Human Genome Project have provided a comprehensive analysis of human DNA, not revealing any dormant strands waiting to be activated.

Epigenetics and Gene Expression

While the concept of "activating" dormant strands of DNA isn't supported by mainstream science, the field of epigenetics does explore how genes can be turned "on" or "off" under specific conditions. Epigenetic mechanisms can lead to changes in gene expression without altering the underlying DNA sequence. Factors such as environment, stress, and even spiritual practices like meditation can influence epigenetic modifications.

Could this be what's referred to as "DNA activation" in spiritual circles? It's a possibility, but one that hasn't been rigorously proven.

Quantum Biology: A New Frontier

Some researchers are venturing into the realm of quantum biology to explore the interaction between quantum mechanics and biological systems. While it's a nascent field, theories like quantum consciousness propose that quantum phenomena could play a role in cognitive processes and possibly even spiritual experiences. However, as of now, this field does not provide any direct evidence supporting the claims about DNA activation specific to starseeds.

Cautions and Considerations

It's essential to approach the subject of DNA activation with an open mind but also a discerning perspective. Claims about activating dormant DNA strands often come packaged with offers for paid services or products like "activation kits," which promise to unlock hidden spiritual potential. Without peer-reviewed evidence supporting these claims, they should be met with skepticism.

Moreover, while spiritual experiences are deeply personal and not easily quantifiable, it's crucial not to conflate spiritual beliefs with established scientific theories. Doing so risks diluting the credibility of both.

Summary

The idea of DNA activation has taken a significant place in discussions surrounding starseeds and their unique capabilities. While the notion of awakening dormant strands of DNA to unlock spiritual or cosmic wisdom is captivating, it is not supported by current scientific understanding. However, the study of epigenetics shows that environmental factors can indeed influence gene expression, albeit not in the way typically described in spiritual teachings. Quantum biology offers another intriguing avenue for future research, but as of now, it doesn't validate claims about DNA activation. Therefore, while keeping an open mind is important, discernment and critical thinking are equally crucial when navigating the complex landscape of spirituality and science.

CHAPTER 20: STARSEED CHILDREN: INDIGOS, CRYSTALS, AND RAINBOWS

In the rich tapestry of starseed experiences, children occupy a particularly enchanting and influential position. Referred to as Indigo, Crystal, and Rainbow children, these young souls are believed to exhibit traits and qualities that not only differentiate them from typical children but also align them more closely with the starseed mission of planetary healing and transformation. This chapter delves into the unique attributes of these starseed children, aiming to shed light on their roles, characteristics, and influence on both earthly and cosmic scales.

Indigo Children: The Trailblazers

Indigo children are generally understood as the first wave of starseed children, appearing prominently in the late 20th century. Their name, "Indigo," is said to be derived from the distinctive indigo aura that surrounds them. These children are often characterized by an innate sense of integrity and a natural tendency to question or defy societal norms. Highly intuitive, they are considered to be old souls who are wise beyond their years. Their primary mission is believed to be one of shaking up outdated systems and breaking down structures that no longer serve humanity's growth.

Psychological traits often attributed to Indigo children include a strong sense of self, independent thinking, and sometimes a perceived stubbornness or rebelliousness. Many are also highly sensitive or empathic, attuned to the emotions and energies of those around them. While these traits may sometimes be misconstrued as behavioral issues, understanding the spiritual context of Indigo children provides a different perspective on their actions and motives.

Crystal Children: The Harmonizers

Arriving after the Indigo wave, Crystal children are often seen as the peacemakers and harmonizers. Their aura is typically described as crystalline, and they are noted for their clear, calm energy. Highly empathic and compassionate, they bring an innate sense of peace and unity to their surroundings. Unlike Indigos, who are more inclined to act as system-busters, Crystal children prefer to create spaces of harmony and coexistence.

Crystal children are often observed to have delayed speech development, not because of any cognitive delays, but because they are believed to communicate more effectively through non-verbal means, especially during their early years. They are known for their telepathic abilities and are considered highly spiritual beings. Their mission aligns with healing—be it emotional, spiritual, or even physical—and they often possess unique abilities in alternative healing modalities from a young age.

Rainbow Children: The Integrators

The most recent category, Rainbow children, are thought to

be born with very little or no karmic baggage, allowing them to navigate the world with ease and joy. Highly creative and constantly energetic, Rainbow children are considered to be the integrators, whose mission is to bring together the best traits of both Indigo and Crystal children while adding their unique attributes to the mix. They are characterized by their extremely loving nature, adaptability, and an inexorable optimism.

Rainbow children are often thought to possess strong wills and even stronger personalities. Unlike their Indigo and Crystal counterparts, they usually grow up in more stable and loving environments, which is believed to facilitate their mission of global healing on a grand scale. Their highly developed psychic abilities, coupled with their loving nature, position them as catalysts for profound social and spiritual transformation.

Contributions and Challenges

Each of these categories of starseed children—Indigo, Crystal, and Rainbow—brings a unique set of qualities and challenges to the earthly experience. While they share the broader starseed mission of planetary transformation, their distinct roles and attributes make them special contributors to this grand undertaking.

However, it's crucial to note that these classifications are not rigid. Not every child fits neatly into one category, and many may exhibit traits that span multiple types. Moreover, as with all spiritual concepts, the notion of Indigo, Crystal, and Rainbow children should be approached with discernment, and preferably personal experience, rather than being accepted as an unequivocal truth.

In summary, Indigo, Crystal, and Rainbow children represent facets of the ongoing starseed mission to bring about planetary healing and spiritual evolution. Their unique attributes and roles serve as different threads in the intricate web of cosmic service, each contributing to the larger tapestry of transformation. Whether you are a parent, educator, or simply someone interested in spiritual evolution, understanding these unique children can offer valuable insights into the future that awaits us—a future filled with promise, complexity, and an ever-expanding cosmic awareness.

CHAPTER 21: STARSEED SYMBOLS AND CODES

Symbols and codes have been a part of human culture for millennia, offering ways to communicate, understand the universe, and connect to higher realms of existence. For starseeds, souls believed to originate from different star systems and incarnated on Earth for specific missions, the role of symbols, codes, and geometric patterns can be particularly resonant. These symbols are not only gateways to deeper understanding but also tools for activation, awakening, and alignment with their cosmic missions.

The Nature of Symbols and Codes

In general, symbols and codes can be considered as condensed packets of information, energy, or intent. They can be simple, like a basic geometric shape, or complex, like intricate mandalas or crop circle designs. In the context of starseeds, these symbols often contain specific frequencies and vibrational patterns that resonate with their unique energetic make-up. They can serve as catalysts for awakening latent abilities, enhancing spiritual insights, and aligning with their star families or origins.

Some commonly used symbols for starseeds include the Flower

of Life, the Merkaba, and the Caduceus. These symbols have often been spotted in various ancient cultures, suggesting a universal appeal or a timeless relevance. While they are not exclusive to starseeds, their presence in starseed circles and literature tends to be significant. The idea is that these symbols, much like cosmic zip files, can unlock layers of understanding, spiritual evolution, and even DNA activation.

Geometric Patterns as Universal Language

Geometry is often considered a universal language, a notion that plays a significant role in the starseed narrative. Geometric forms like the Platonic solids are thought to be the building blocks of the universe, representing elemental constructs like earth, water, air, fire, and ether. For starseeds, engaging with these geometric forms can facilitate a deeper connection with the very fabric of the cosmos.

Sacred geometry, including complex designs like the Flower of Life or simpler forms like the circle or the triangle, can provide starseeds with a kind of cosmic map or key. These shapes and patterns can help in visualization exercises, meditation, or other spiritual practices aimed at elevating consciousness, opening interstellar communication channels, or healing.

Numerical Codes and Their Significance

Apart from geometric forms and symbols, numerical sequences also hold particular significance for starseeds. Angel numbers like 1111, 2222, or sequences like the Fibonacci series, can be seen as messages from the universe or their star families. While the interpretation of these numbers can be subjective, many starseeds find that encountering these numbers frequently is a form of synchronicity that provides guidance, affirmation, or caution.

Light Language and Star Scripts

Some starseeds report encountering or channeling scripts, alphabets, or symbols that don't correspond to any known earthly language. Often referred to as "light language," these scripts are said to convey higher-dimensional wisdom and can be either written, spoken, or even sung. The comprehension of light language is less about literal translation and more about intuitive understanding. The symbols or words are said to activate dormant DNA or facilitate higher-level healing, bypassing the intellectual mind and directly interacting with the soul or energetic body.

Practical Applications

Starseeds can use these symbols and codes in a variety of ways to aid their earthly missions and spiritual journeys. Whether it's through meditation focused on a particular symbol, using numerical sequences in daily life as affirmation or guidance, or integrating geometric shapes into art and design, the possibilities are plentiful. Some also opt for tattoos or wear jewelry featuring these symbols as a constant reminder and activator of their cosmic origins and purposes.

In conclusion, the realm of symbols, codes, and geometric patterns offers a rich tapestry of possibilities for starseeds. While not unique to them, these elements provide specific resonance and utility in the context of their cosmic origins and earthly missions. Whether as tools for awakening, keys to cosmic wisdom, or catalysts for deeper spiritual practice, these symbols serve as versatile and potent allies on the starseed journey.

CHAPTER 22: CHANNELING AND MEDIUMSHIP: ACCESSING HIGHER REALMS

Introduction

After exploring various facets of the starseed experience—from galactic origins to earthly roles—it's essential to delve into how starseeds can deepen their connection to higher-dimensional beings and energies. One way to accomplish this is through the practices of channeling and mediumship. Although these concepts are often mentioned in spiritual and esoteric discussions, their role in the life of a starseed can be particularly impactful. This chapter will guide you through the essence, methodologies, and significance of channeling and mediumship as tools for starseeds seeking to connect with their galactic roots.

The Essence of Channeling and Mediumship

Channeling is the practice of becoming a conduit for information, messages, or energies from non-physical sources, often described as higher-dimensional beings, spirit guides, or ascended masters.

In contrast, mediumship typically focuses on communicating with the spirits of those who have passed on. Both practices require a state of heightened intuition and receptivity. For starseeds, channeling can be a way to connect with their star families, receive guidance for their earthly missions, and even access cosmic wisdom.

Mediumship, although more often associated with communication with departed human souls, can also be a tool for starseeds to connect with energies that help them understand their earthly roles better. While channeling usually entails receiving information for a broader purpose, mediumship often focuses on delivering messages of a personal nature, often offering comfort, closure, or guidance.

Methods of Channeling

Several methods of channeling exist, each with its own set of practices and precautions. Some of the most commonly utilized methods among starseeds and spiritual seekers include:

- Trance Channeling: In this method, the channeler enters a trance state, allowing another consciousness to speak through them. The channeler often has no memory of the messages relayed during the trance.

- Conscious Channeling: Unlike trance channeling, the channeler remains conscious and aware during the process. They may receive messages as thoughts, feelings, or even visions, which they then translate into language.

- Automatic Writing: In this form of channeling, the individual allows their hand to move freely across the paper, writing down messages without consciously thinking about them.

- Clairaudient Channeling: This method involves receiving messages through inner hearing. The channeler hears the messages and then relays them.

Precautions and Ethical Considerations

Channeling and mediumship require a high level of discernment. Not all sources reached through these practices are benevolent or aligned with your highest good. Before engaging in these activities, many experienced practitioners recommend grounding techniques, setting up protective energetic boundaries, and explicitly stating the intent to connect only with beings of the highest light and wisdom.

Ethically, it's also crucial to handle the messages received responsibly. If you're sharing messages with others, ensure you have their consent, and make it clear that channeling is a spiritual practice subject to interpretation.

Significance for Starseeds

For starseeds, channeling and mediumship can be more than just spiritual practices; they can be pathways to deeper understanding and clearer guidance. Connecting with higher-dimensional beings can offer insights into their galactic origins and even unlock information that assists in their earthly missions. Some starseeds find that their innate abilities in these practices awaken more fully as they go through their awakening process, allowing them a clearer channel to cosmic wisdom.

Mediumship can help starseeds understand the cycles of life, death, and rebirth, further emphasizing the interconnectedness of all things. Through channeling, starseeds can receive new healing modalities, spiritual technologies, or wisdom teachings that they can then integrate into their lives and share with others.

Summary

Channeling and mediumship serve as fascinating spiritual tools, particularly enriching for those identifying as starseeds. Whether it's connecting with higher-dimensional beings or understanding the nuances of life and death, these practices offer a rich tapestry of experiences and insights. By understanding the methods and ethical considerations involved, starseeds can engage in these practices responsibly and fruitfully. With proper guidance and discernment, these ancient spiritual practices can become a vital part of a starseed's journey, enabling them to deepen their understanding of both their galactic heritage and their earthly mission.

CHAPTER 23: THE LAW OF ONE AND STARSEEDS

The Law of One is a philosophical and spiritual framework that has gained significant attention in metaphysical communities. Often discussed in the context of channeled material and cosmic wisdom, the Law of One has interesting implications for understanding the role and mission of starseeds. In this chapter, we will delve into the core tenets of the Law of One and explore how it dovetails with the notion of starseeds, their purpose, and their interaction with the greater universe.

Core Tenets of the Law of One

The Law of One is often articulated through a series of channeled messages claimed to be from a collective consciousness known as Ra. Although the source may be debated, the philosophical wisdom contained in these texts has resonated with many. At the heart of this philosophy is the notion that all is one and one is all —that everything in the universe is interconnected and part of a singular, infinite Creator. It posits that every soul is on a journey of evolution, progressing through various densities or levels of consciousness, seeking to return to the oneness from which it originated.

Another critical aspect of the Law of One is the idea of polarity and the balance between service-to-self and service-to-others orientations. According to this view, souls can evolve through either of these paths, but service-to-others is often seen as more aligned with the unity consciousness, fostering spiritual growth at a quicker pace.

Starseeds and the Journey of Evolution

The Law of One's concept of soul evolution through various densities seems to align with the starseed narrative. Starseeds are believed to be souls that have originated from higher densities or dimensions and have incarnated on Earth to assist in its collective evolution. In the context of the Law of One, starseeds might be viewed as souls that have advanced through service-to-others orientation and are here to facilitate Earth's transition from a third-density reality focused on individual consciousness to a fourth-density reality centered on group consciousness.

Starseeds often report feeling different, misunderstood, or alienated because they instinctively operate from a place of unity consciousness. They find themselves driven towards service-to-others and are intuitively attuned to the interconnectedness of all life. This innate understanding can be seen as evidence of their soul's journey through higher densities, which echoes the evolutionary trajectory described in the Law of One.

Polarity and Purpose

The Law of One's concept of polarity also holds significance for starseeds. As they are often motivated by a service-to-others orientation, starseeds may find that their missions involve helping humanity transcend its service-to-self tendencies. This could involve a range of activities, from grassroots activism to offering spiritual teachings aimed at elevating collective consciousness. The point is to assist in balancing the planetary polarity, nudging it closer to a service-to-others paradigm. This is an essential facet of their earthly missions and one that complements the broader themes within the Law of One.

Ethical and Moral Implications

The Law of One also explores the ethical and moral aspects of existence, emphasizing the significance of free will. Starseeds must exercise their free will responsibly and with discernment, ensuring that their actions align with their service-to-others orientation. Furthermore, they are often confronted with the ethical challenge of respecting the free will of others, even when they disagree with service-to-self orientations. This requires a profound understanding of the Law of One's principles, emphasizing the balance between intervention and non-interference.

The Law of One and the Collective Mission

Finally, the Law of One teaches that we are collectively moving toward the remembrance of unity and the acknowledgment of the singular divine source. Starseeds, being an integral part of this cosmic tapestry, are not just individually fulfilling their missions but contributing to a grander, collective purpose. Their work—whether it be healing, teaching, or inspiring—is aimed at accelerating the journey towards oneness, as dictated by the Law of One.

In summary, the Law of One provides a philosophical framework that can enrich our understanding of starseeds, offering a deeper perspective on their earthly missions and cosmic origins. It speaks to the heart of what many starseeds feel instinctively: that they are here to serve, to uplift, and to help guide humanity through a critical juncture in its evolutionary path. Through this lens, the Law of One serves not just as a philosophy but as a roadmap, helping starseeds navigate the complex terrains of ethical dilemmas, spiritual missions, and the ultimate quest for unity.

CHAPTER 24: FAMOUS STARSEEDS: REAL-LIFE EXAMPLES

The topic of starseeds has fascinated people for years, encompassing both the metaphysical and, more recently, the mainstream. While many individuals claim to have unique spiritual experiences that align with the starseed narrative, there are also those who have captured the public eye. This chapter profiles individuals who have either claimed to be starseeds or have been identified as such by the community, aiming to dissect their life missions and contributions.

Public Figures and Starseed Identification

It's important to note that starseed identification for public figures often comes from either self-proclamation or the interpretation by followers rather than scientific evidence. These identifications can be contentious, open to interpretation, and may not be universally accepted. Nevertheless, there is an intriguing range of influential people, from artists to spiritual teachers, who have been labeled as starseeds.

Nikola Tesla, an inventor and futurist famous for his contributions to the construction of the contemporary alternating current (AC) electrical delivery system, is an example that comes up quite frequently. Even while Tesla himself never made the assertion that he was a starseed, members of the starseed community have hypothesized that his superior understanding of energy and frequency could be indications that he came from a starseed family. His desire to provide free energy to the world has been considered by some as a mission aligned with typical starseed goals of advancing human civilization.

Contemporary Starseeds in Alternative Communities

Within the realm of spiritual and metaphysical communities, some individuals openly identify as starseeds and make it a part of their life mission to educate others about it. These individuals often become spiritual teachers, healers, or authors who aim to help awaken other starseeds or lightworkers. Such contemporary starseeds often have a strong online presence, leveraging social media platforms, and websites to reach a global audience.

The content they produce often explores starseed traits, the awakening process, and techniques for alignment with one's cosmic mission. While their teachings may not be mainstream, they offer invaluable insights for those deeply entrenched in starseed philosophy.

The Entertainment Industry

The entertainment industry is another area where the concept of starseeds has gained some traction. Several musicians, actors, and artists have either openly claimed to be starseeds or have woven starseed-like themes into their work. For example, musicians in the New Age or metaphysical genres often create compositions aimed at facilitating spiritual awakening or healing, elements commonly associated with starseeds.

Such artistic contributions are notable for their potential to reach large audiences and subtly influence collective consciousness. Through their creative works, these artists often manage to spark curiosity and introduce metaphysical concepts to people who might otherwise not encounter them.

Skepticism and Consideration

Despite the compelling narratives around famous starseeds, there is a level of skepticism that must be acknowledged. No empirical evidence can definitively prove the cosmic origin of any individual. Often, the labeling of public figures as starseeds is subjective, based on the interpretation of their work, statements, or life missions through a starseed lens.

As such, when considering any public figure as a starseed, it's important to approach the topic with an open mind yet maintain a discerning attitude. Evaluating the impact of their contributions on humanity, or how closely their life missions align with common starseed attributes, can offer some perspective. However, definitive conclusions remain elusive, leaving room for personal interpretation and belief.

Summary

The concept of famous starseeds serves as a fascinating point of intersection between the mystical and the mainstream. While some figures are posthumously interpreted as starseeds due to their contributions to humanity, others openly claim their cosmic heritage and work to awaken similar traits in the general populace. Though the identification of public figures as starseeds is often speculative and subjective, the discussion it sparks can serve as a gateway for many into the broader realm of starseed

CAMPBELL QUINN MCCARTHY

philosophy and cosmic consciousness.

CHAPTER 25: GALACTIC LANGUAGES AND LIGHT CODES

The experience of being a starseed is often filled with a range of phenomena that could be classified as extraordinary or even otherworldly. One of these phenomena that has caught the fascination of many in the starseed community is the concept of galactic languages and light codes. These are channeled forms of communication said to come from higher dimensions or extraterrestrial origins. In this chapter, we will delve into the intricacies of galactic languages and light codes, their relevance, and their applicability in the life of a starseed.

What Are Galactic Languages?

Galactic languages are channeled forms of communication that some individuals claim to speak or write spontaneously, often during moments of deep meditation, altered states of consciousness, or spiritual experiences. They are often incomprehensible to the human ear and mind but are said to carry frequencies of light and sound that resonate at higher dimensional levels. The languages may be vocalized, written down as scripts, or even visualized as geometric patterns. They are thought to facilitate a direct communication link between the starseed and their star family or higher-dimensional beings.

The Significance of Light Codes

Light codes are often closely related to galactic languages but are usually expressed in visual or geometric forms. These could be patterns, symbols, or configurations that appear in one's mind's eye, in dreams, or even in physical manifestations. Light codes are thought to hold encrypted information that can activate dormant DNA, enhance spiritual growth, and accelerate the awakening process. Some starseeds work with light codes by drawing or visualizing them during meditation to unlock their hidden potential or receive guidance.

Scientific Perspectives

It's important to note that while the starseed community and some spiritual traditions place great importance on galactic languages and light codes, mainstream science generally does not recognize these phenomena. Linguistic studies usually focus on languages that have syntax, semantics, and shared meanings, none of which galactic languages possess in a way that can be universally analyzed. Similarly, the concept of light codes activating dormant DNA does not have scientific backing, although research in epigenetics has begun to explore how beliefs and experiences can affect gene expression.

How Do Starseeds Use Them?

Starseeds who resonate with galactic languages or light codes often integrate them into their spiritual practices. Some report that speaking these languages during meditation deepens their states of consciousness. Others feel that drawing or visualizing light codes helps them align more closely with their galactic origins. Some even incorporate these elements into their healing work, believing that the frequencies carried by these languages and codes can facilitate emotional and physical healing.

Controversies and Considerations

While many find value in galactic languages and light codes, it's essential to approach them with discernment. There is a risk of veering into the realms of fantasy or delusion if these experiences aren't grounded in some form of personal verification or community validation. Also, some skeptics argue that these languages and codes could be products of the subconscious mind rather than transmissions from higher dimensions. Moreover, while some starseeds feel empowered by these experiences, it is crucial to remember that they are not substitutes for grounded, earthly responsibilities and interpersonal relationships.

In summary, galactic languages and light codes offer a compelling and mysterious avenue for exploration within the starseed community. Whether viewed as bridges to higher dimensions or intricate aspects of the human psyche, they add another layer of complexity to the multifaceted experience of being a starseed. While the scientific community has yet to acknowledge these phenomena, many starseeds find them to be invaluable tools for spiritual growth, self-discovery, and cosmic connection. As with any spiritual practice or experience, the key is to approach them with an open mind but also a discerning heart, carefully navigating the fine line between cosmic curiosity and grounded reality.

CHAPTER 26: SACRED GEOMETRY: THE BLUEPRINT OF CREATION

Sacred geometry has been a topic of fascination across cultures and eras, often seen as the blueprint of creation itself. For starseeds, this subject takes on added significance as it is believed to hold keys to understanding both their galactic origins and their earthly missions. This chapter delves into the intricate world of sacred geometry, exploring its fundamental concepts, its historical lineage, and its particular relevance for starseeds.

The Foundations of Sacred Geometry

The study of geometric shapes and proportions that reoccur throughout the universe, from the microcosm of atomic structures to the macrocosm of celestial bodies, is what is referred to as sacred geometry. Basic geometric shapes like circles, triangles, and spirals are thought to form the building blocks of all creation. For example, the Fibonacci sequence, a series of numbers in which each number is the sum of the two preceding ones, manifests in nature in phenomena like the spiral arrangement of leaves and the shape of galaxies. Similarly, the Platonic solids, named after the ancient Greek philosopher Plato, are polyhedra that have been studied for their symmetrical beauty and mathematical precision.

A Historical Perspective

The principles of sacred geometry are not new; they have been documented and explored in various civilizations. The Egyptian pyramids, for instance, display a remarkable understanding of geometric principles. In Hindu and Buddhist philosophy, geometric designs known as Yantras and Mandalas have been used for meditation and understanding the nature of existence. The Renaissance saw a revival of interest in geometry, notably expressed in the works of artists like Leonardo da Vinci, who incorporated geometric forms into his art as representations of the divine.

Starseeds and Sacred Geometry

For starseeds, sacred geometry serves as a resonant reminder of their cosmic lineage. The geometric shapes that frequently appear in crop circles, for example, have been interpreted by some in the starseed community as messages from their star families. The Merkaba, a shape composed of interlocking tetrahedra, is often associated with the energy fields around the human body and is thought to have special significance for starseeds.

On a practical level, sacred geometry can be employed in daily life for various purposes. Geometric symbols and structures can be used in meditation or to amplify the energy of living spaces. The Flower of Life, a design made up of multiple evenly-spaced, overlapping circles, is a popular geometric figure used for these purposes. Some starseeds also incorporate geometric symbols into their healing practices; for example, using crystal grids arranged in specific geometric shapes to channel energy more effectively.

Unlocking Cosmic Wisdom

Sacred geometry is more than just a set of aesthetically pleasing designs; it's thought to be a language through which cosmic wisdom can be communicated. The complex geometric designs found in fractals, for instance, represent an infinitely repeating pattern across different scales, reflecting the concept of "as above, so below." This idea resonates with many starseeds as it echoes their belief in the interconnectedness of all life, across both earthly and cosmic dimensions.

Understanding the principles of sacred geometry can also be seen as unlocking a kind of universal wisdom. Just as mathematical laws underpin the workings of the universe, so does the symbolic language of geometry offer insights into the deeper order of things. By engaging with sacred geometry, starseeds may find clues to their cosmic origins and missions, embedded in the very fabric of space and time.

Integrating Sacred Geometry into Daily Life

The principles of sacred geometry can be integrated into daily routines and spiritual practices to amplify energies and bring greater awareness. Techniques include meditating on specific shapes like the Flower of Life, setting up geometrically arranged crystal grids for energy work, or even incorporating these shapes into art and home decor. By surrounding themselves with these universal patterns, starseeds can more easily align with their cosmic purposes and perhaps even receive intuitive insights or messages from their galactic families.

In summary, sacred geometry serves as a profound and universal language that can offer starseeds unique insights into their cosmic origins and earthly roles. Whether through meditation, healing practices, or a deeper understanding of the universe's structure, engaging with sacred geometry can be a richly rewarding avenue for starseeds navigating their earthly journey while seeking to fulfill their cosmic missions.

CHAPTER 27: SOUL CONTRACTS AND FREE WILL: THE STARSEED DILEMMA

One of the most nuanced and complicated aspects of the starseed experience revolves around the concept of soul contracts and how they intersect with the principle of free will. This chapter aims to delve into this rich topic, exploring how starseeds navigate the tension between predetermined missions and personal choices.

The Nature of Soul Contracts

Soul contracts are considered to be spiritual agreements that a soul makes before incarnating on Earth. In the context of starseeds, these agreements often outline specific missions or roles that the individual is supposed to fulfill. The terms of a soul contract might involve spreading awareness about spirituality, contributing to ecological conservation, or even catalyzing change in societal structures.

While these contracts serve as a guiding framework, they don't usually provide a minute-by-minute itinerary. The details of how one accomplishes the objectives set forth in a soul contract are usually left open, which is where free will comes into play.

Free Will: The Power of Choice

The concept of free will asserts that individuals have the power to make choices that are neither determined by natural causality nor predestined by fate. In the context of starseeds, this implies the freedom to navigate their earthly journey in a manner of their own choosing, even if a larger mission or purpose has been outlined for them.

This freedom can manifest in myriad ways: a starseed might choose to abandon their mission temporarily or even completely, opt for a different spiritual path, or employ unconventional methods to fulfill their objectives. Such decisions can have implications not only for the individual starseed but also for their soul group or even the larger collective mission of starseeds on Earth.

The Interplay between Destiny and Choice

For a starseed, the intersection of soul contracts and free will creates a fascinating dynamic. On one hand, there's a guiding blueprint—the soul contract—that outlines their overarching mission. On the other hand, they have the autonomy to make choices that could diverge from or align with that mission. This creates a constantly shifting landscape where destiny and choice coalesce in unpredictable ways.

Consider an analogy: if the soul contract is like a map of a city, free will represents the various routes one can take to reach a destination within that city. The map provides the general layout, but the streets one chooses, the stops one makes, and the pace one maintains are all up to individual discretion.

Balancing Commitment and Flexibility

The key for starseeds, then, lies in balancing the guiding principles outlined in their soul contracts with the freedom and flexibility that come with free will. This often involves a lot of introspection, meditation, and sometimes consultation with divinatory tools or spiritual guides to understand the best course of action at any given time.

While a soul contract can offer a sense of purpose and direction, it should not be viewed as a limiting document but rather as a foundational guide. Understanding that they can exercise free will allows starseeds to bring a level of creativity and personal touch to their missions, making the journey as enriching as the destination.

Ethical Considerations and Personal Responsibility

When discussing soul contracts and free will, ethical considerations inevitably surface. How responsible are starseeds for fulfilling their soul contracts? What happens if they deviate from their predestined path? While there are varying viewpoints on this, most spiritual philosophies advocate for a balanced approach, where personal responsibility is honored but not to the extent that it becomes a source of guilt or emotional burden.

In essence, while the soul contract provides a mission, the starseed is not generally considered 'bound' to it in a manner that negates personal choice or ethical considerations. It's about harmonizing one's cosmic mission with personal values and choices, taking into account the interconnectedness of all actions and their consequences, both in earthly and cosmic dimensions.

In summary, the interplay between soul contracts and free will is a complex but enriching aspect of the starseed experience. While soul contracts provide a framework for their cosmic missions, free will allows starseeds the latitude to explore, adapt, and even redefine their paths. Balancing the two involves ethical considerations, personal responsibility, and an open heart, making the journey not just a cosmic obligation but a deeply personal spiritual quest.

CHAPTER 28: STARSEEDS AND EARTH'S HISTORY

The idea that souls from other star systems—often referred to as starseeds—have played an influential role in Earth's history is fascinating and rich with possibilities. According to various esoteric teachings, starseeds have been present during key moments, guiding humanity in ways that are both tangible and subtle. While these concepts are not supported by mainstream academic history, they offer intriguing perspectives when examined through the lens of alternative spirituality.

Prehistoric Times: The First Arrivals

Esoteric teachings suggest that starseeds first arrived on Earth during its early developmental stages. Some speculate that they were involved in the seeding of life itself, while others believe they played a role in the advancement of civilizations. Ideas abound that they assisted in the construction of ancient megalithic structures like Stonehenge or the pyramids of Giza, whose methods of construction still puzzle researchers.

Civilization Milestones: Catalysts of Change

Starseeds are thought to have played roles during significant shifts in human civilization. They are often portrayed as teachers, advisors, or even rulers, imparting wisdom or technologies that led to leaps in human capabilities. For example, the concept of zero in mathematics, the principles of astronomy, or advancements in medicine are often attributed to these cosmic visitors in esoteric circles. While there is no empirical evidence to prove these claims, the theories provide food for thought about how certain revolutionary ideas came into being.

Spiritual Teachers and Philosophers: Guiding Human Consciousness

In various spiritual circles, historical figures who've had a monumental impact on human consciousness are sometimes identified as starseeds. Figures like Buddha, Jesus, and Socrates, who introduced revolutionary spiritual concepts and ethical systems, are occasionally speculated to be starseeds. While such notions are not part of orthodox religious or historical narratives, the idea that these teachers could have had cosmic origins is a recurring theme in esoteric discussions.

Global Crises: Agents of Healing

According to some beliefs, starseeds have a knack for appearing during times of crisis, offering various forms of assistance. Whether it's the collapse of civilizations, major wars, or catastrophic events, the starseeds' role is often seen as that of healers or mediators. For instance, during the dark ages, it's speculated that they helped preserve knowledge that would later be critical for the renaissance. Again, these perspectives are not historically validated but offer an alternative viewpoint on the mysterious elements and coincidences that litter our history.

Modern Times: Harbingers of a New Age

As we move into more recent times, the idea is that starseeds are incarnating more frequently, preparing humanity for a significant evolutionary leap in consciousness. While these ideas are generally not part of mainstream discussions, they are commonly discussed in New Age and spiritual communities. Proponents suggest that starseeds today are involved in various fields such as science, spirituality, environmentalism, and social justice, acting as catalysts for positive change.

Summary

The notion that starseeds have been intricately involved in Earth's history is a captivating subject that resonates with people who are open to esoteric or spiritual perspectives. While there's no mainstream historical or scientific evidence to support these views, they offer a fascinating alternative lens through which to explore the mysteries and coincidences of our past. From the early seeding of life on Earth to the rise and fall of civilizations, and through pivotal moments in spiritual and philosophical development, starseeds are envisioned as cosmic companions on humanity's long journey through time. Whether or not one subscribes to these views, they undeniably provide a rich tapestry of ideas that challenge our understanding of history and our place in the cosmos.

CHAPTER 29: WANDERERS AND WALK-INS: OTHER TYPES OF STARSEEDS

The narrative of starseeds and their cosmic missions usually involves the notion of souls incarnating from other star systems into human forms here on Earth. However, within this broad framework, there are unique modes of incarnation that deserve our attention—Wanderers and Walk-ins. These types of starseeds have particular characteristics that differentiate them from the general starseed population, and their presence on Earth involves distinct circumstances and missions.

Wanderers: The Cosmic Nomads

Wanderers are souls who voluntarily come from higher dimensions or other star systems to assist Earth and its inhabitants. Unlike typical starseeds who incarnate with the primary objective of experiencing Earthly life while fulfilling a mission, Wanderers often come with a focused agenda to serve humanity. They may be advanced souls with a wealth of cosmic wisdom, arriving during times of significant shifts or crises to lend their expertise and energy to Earthly causes.

It's important to note that Wanderers sometimes struggle with "spiritual amnesia," forgetting their cosmic origins and missions. This is considered a necessary challenge to ensure that they engage authentically with the human experience, enabling them to assist Earth from a grounded perspective. As they awaken, they may experience an intense sense of homesickness or feel out of place before finally coming into the understanding of their true origins and objectives.

Walk-ins: The Soul Exchangers

Walk-ins present an even more intriguing scenario. A Walk-in experience happens when one soul exits a human body, allowing another soul to "walk into" the body and take over. This typically occurs by mutual agreement and is often pre-arranged before either soul incarnates. The soul that walks in usually has a specific mission that requires a human body but does not necessarily require a full human lifespan to complete.

For the person experiencing a Walk-in, the transition may manifest as a sudden change in personality, preferences, and even skills. It's not uncommon for them to undergo drastic lifestyle changes, such as shifting careers or ending long-term relationships, as they align with the new soul's mission. While the concept of Walk-ins might stretch conventional understanding, it is discussed in various metaphysical circles as a legitimate experience.

The Complexity of Identifying Wanderers and Walk-ins

Identifying Wanderers and Walk-ins can be a complicated task. Often, they themselves are unaware of their status until they go through a significant awakening process. Some signs may include a sudden influx of psychic or healing abilities, unexplainable memories or dreams of other worlds and lifetimes, or a deep, innate understanding of cosmic laws and spiritual principles.

As with other types of starseeds, validation often comes through personal revelation or synchronistic events that trigger the awakening of their cosmic identity. Some may also find clarity through spiritual guidance, either from intuitive practitioners or through their own connection to higher-dimensional beings.

The Missions: Earthly and Cosmic Roles

The missions of Wanderers and Walk-ins are as varied as those of other starseeds, although they tend to lean more toward crisis intervention and global transformation. Wanderers often focus on sharing wisdom, healing, and facilitating spiritual awakenings, aiming to raise Earth's vibrational frequency. Walk-ins may be more task-oriented, coming in to accomplish specific missions that contribute to both earthly and cosmic evolutions.

It's worth noting that despite the apparent urgency of their missions, free will remains paramount. Wanderers and Walk-ins have the freedom to align with their missions or choose another path. Like all starseeds, they are not exempt from the challenges and distractions of earthly life, and their ultimate success in fulfilling their missions is not guaranteed.

Synergies and Collaborations

Interestingly, Wanderers and Walk-ins often find themselves collaborating with other starseeds, lightworkers, and spiritually awakened humans. These alliances are often formed spontaneously, guided by higher-dimensional orchestration or what some may term "divine timing."

In summary, Wanderers and Walk-ins add another layer of complexity and diversity to our understanding of starseeds. While they share the overarching mission of service to humanity and Earth, their unique modes of incarnation and specific roles contribute to a richer tapestry of cosmic interaction. Whether through sharing wisdom or engaging in task-specific missions, these special types of starseeds play an integral role in Earth's spiritual and evolutionary journey.

CHAPTER 30: LIGHTWORKERS VS. STARSEEDS: SIMILARITIES AND DIFFERENCES

The terms "Lightworker" and "Starseed" are often used interchangeably within spiritual circles, creating a layer of confusion for those new to these concepts or even for those who have some grounding in them. While both groups share the overarching mission of aiding humanity and Earth, their origins, focus, and skillsets often diverge. This chapter aims to clarify the differences and similarities between Lightworkers and Starseeds, offering a nuanced understanding of these two distinct yet interconnected roles.

Galactic Roots and Earthly Origins

Starseeds, as discussed in earlier chapters, are believed to originate from different star systems like Pleiades, Arcturus, and Sirius. Their souls incarnate on Earth with specific missions to assist in global and cosmic evolution. The concept hinges on the idea of a soul's journey across multiple lifetimes and dimensions, sometimes beyond Earth.

Lightworkers, on the other hand, may or may not have a cosmic origin. Their primary focus lies in raising Earth's vibrations and aiding humanity's spiritual development. While some Lightworkers may identify as Starseeds, others may consider themselves purely Earthly beings. Therefore, the concept of Lightworkers is a bit more flexible when it comes to the origin of the soul.

Focus and Mission

Both Lightworkers and Starseeds have missions centered around service to others, but the nuances of these missions can differ. Starseeds often bring in advanced knowledge, wisdom, and capabilities from their home star systems. Their roles may involve ushering in new technologies, promoting ecological sustainability, or providing spiritual enlightenment—tasks that assist in Earth's transition into higher dimensions of consciousness.

Lightworkers generally concentrate on healing, teaching, and guiding individuals and communities on Earth. Their skillsets are often more tailored to Earthly challenges, from social injustice to environmental degradation. They may excel in roles such as counselors, environmentalists, teachers, or spiritual guides.

Unique Skill Sets and Tools

Starseeds often possess skills that seem otherworldly or highly advanced. They may have an affinity for technology, an intuitive understanding of energy work, or a knack for perceiving higher-dimensional realities. These unique abilities often align with their cosmic missions, enabling them to act as bridges between Earth and other star systems.

Lightworkers might not always display such exotic abilities. Their skills are often more grounded, such as the capability for empathic understanding, teaching, or physical healing. Many Lightworkers are drawn to professions like social work, psychology, and various forms of therapy.

Interconnected Yet Individual Roles

It's essential to recognize that while all Starseeds can be Lightworkers, not all Lightworkers are Starseeds. Starseeds usually have a broader cosmic mission that encompasses Lightwork but goes beyond it. They often work on multi-dimensional levels and may be more attuned to cosmic shifts and galactic alignments.

Lightworkers may focus more on the here and now, addressing the immediate needs of Earth and its inhabitants. However, their work is no less critical. Their Earth-centered approach often provides the grounded energy needed to implement the grand visions brought by Starseeds.

Integrating Both Aspects

Some individuals may identify as both a Lightworker and a Starseed, integrating aspects of both roles. For example, a Starseed with a mission to introduce new healing modalities to Earth may take on the Lightworker role of a healer or therapist. Similarly, a Lightworker focused on social justice may discover a broader cosmic mission that resonates with Starseed attributes, expanding their focus to include issues like global unity or even cosmic peace.

In summary, while Starseeds and Lightworkers share the common goal of elevating Earthly and human consciousness, they often differ in their origins, primary focus, and unique skill sets. Starseeds tend to have a broader, more cosmic mission, with skills that can seem otherworldly. Lightworkers, meanwhile, often focus on Earth-based service, with abilities more aligned with immediate Earthly challenges. Understanding these nuances can help individuals better identify their roles and missions, facilitating more effective and harmonious work in aiding both Earth and the broader cosmos.

CHAPTER 31: STARSEEDS AND SPIRITUAL TRADITIONS

Starseeds are often associated with specific star systems or cosmic origins, but their influence can be traced across various spiritual traditions and practices on Earth. This chapter delves into the interplay between starseed philosophies and earthly spiritual traditions. It aims to elucidate how elements of various spiritual systems resonate with the core beliefs of starseeds, and conversely, how starseed ideologies might shed new light on these ancient practices.

The Eastern Traditions: Hinduism and Buddhism

In Eastern philosophies like Hinduism and Buddhism, the concept of reincarnation is a fundamental tenet. These traditions hold the belief in a cycle of birth, death, and rebirth, known as samsara. This resonates with the starseed idea of incarnating across multiple lifetimes and realms for the purpose of soul evolution. The Hindu concept of Atman, or the inner self, shares similarities with the starseed notion of a soul carrying wisdom from multiple star systems.

Buddhism's emphasis on compassion and interconnectedness also aligns well with the starseed mission of raising collective consciousness. The Buddhist teachings on bodhisattvas, or enlightened beings who choose to remain in the cycle of reincarnation to help others, can be viewed as a terrestrial echo of the starseed commitment to aid in Earth's evolution.

The Western Traditions: Christianity and Judaism

In Western spiritual traditions like Christianity and Judaism, there are mystical subsets that share synergies with starseed thought. The concept of angels, for instance, as messengers or protectors from a higher realm, is in some ways analogous to the starseed archetype. Kabbalistic texts, which explore the mystical aspects of Judaism, discuss the Sefirot or divine emanations, that might be interpreted as cosmic energy centers, akin to the chakras that starseeds are believed to have.

Christian mysticism, with its emphasis on transcendent experiences and communion with the divine, has thematic overlaps with the starseed focus on higher-dimensional consciousness. The concept of 'Kingdom of Heaven within' in Christian teachings can be paralleled to the idea of internal cosmic alignment within a starseed.

Indigenous Beliefs: Shamanism and Animism

Indigenous cultures often contain spiritual practices that reverberate with starseed beliefs. Shamanistic traditions, for instance, frequently involve the practitioner traveling to other realms to gain wisdom or healing capabilities. This mirrors the starseed concept of drawing on knowledge from other dimensions or star systems. Animistic beliefs in the sanctity of nature and the interconnectedness of all life forms resonate strongly with starseed ideologies that often emphasize ecological stewardship and unity consciousness.

New Age and Modern Spirituality

Modern spiritual movements have been particularly receptive to starseed ideas. The New Age spirituality often integrates a blend of ancient wisdom traditions, metaphysical beliefs, and cosmic spirituality, thereby making it a fertile ground for the expansion of starseed concepts. Practices like channeling, use of crystals, and aura reading are commonly endorsed both within New Age circles and starseed communities.

Sufism and Mystical Islam

In Sufism, the mystical branch of Islam, the idea of a universal soul and the quest for divine love are emphasized. Rumi, the famed Sufi poet, often wrote about the soul's desire to return to a divine source, which can be likened to a starseed's yearning for their star family or point of origin. The Sufi practices of meditation and ecstatic dance as a way to commune with the divine also share similarities with starseed practices aimed at raising vibrational frequencies.

Summary

Various spiritual traditions across the globe exhibit striking parallels with starseed beliefs and practices. From reincarnation in Eastern religions to the mysticism in Western and Islamic traditions, and from the shamanic journeys in indigenous cultures to modern New Age practices, the imprints of starseed philosophies are discernible. Understanding these intersections not only enriches our comprehension of starseed ideologies but also amplifies the universal themes in humanity's diverse spiritual traditions. It presents a compelling case for the interconnected tapestry of spiritual wisdom and cosmic lore, inviting us to explore this rich and complex field further.

CHAPTER 32: THE SHADOW SIDE: PITFALLS AND MISCONCEPTIONS

The journey of understanding starseeds, their galactic origins, and their earthly missions is awe-inspiring and full of uplifting possibilities. However, like any topic that deals with spiritual or metaphysical issues, the concept of starseeds is not without its pitfalls and misconceptions. These stumbling blocks can sometimes hinder the understanding or the spiritual growth of those who are involved in this community. Let's take a deeper look into some of these challenges.

Spiritual Bypassing

The danger of spiritually ignoring one's responsibilities is a key issue that exists among the starseed community. The use of one's spiritual beliefs in order to avoid facing unresolved emotional issues or psychological scars is the practice that is referred to by this word. Because starseeds often consider themselves to be spiritually awakened souls with a cosmic mission, there may be a temptation to overlook human frailties and emotional needs. The thought pattern could be something like, "I'm a highly evolved being from Arcturus; why should I worry about my earthly troubles?" This can lead to a neglect of practical, earthly responsibilities or unresolved emotional issues, which is not conducive for anyone's spiritual growth, let alone fulfilling any supposed cosmic mission.

The Narcissism Trap

Another concern is the unintentional fostering of narcissistic tendencies. The idea of being a starseed can be incredibly empowering. Knowing that you might have a cosmic lineage can instill a sense of purpose or destiny. However, this newfound sense of "specialness" can sometimes inflate the ego, fostering a belief that one is superior to others who are not identified as starseeds. This attitude can be harmful, not just to the individual but also to the community and the collective spiritual journey.

Misuse of Terminology

The language surrounding starseeds is rich and poetic, filled with terms like "galactic heritage," "light codes," and "5D reality." While these can serve as empowering metaphors and can indeed be profoundly meaningful to some, there's a risk of these terms being misunderstood or misapplied. Without a grounded understanding, these phrases can become mere buzzwords that dilute the genuine experiences or sentiments they aim to describe.

The "Savior" Complex

The notion that starseeds are here on a cosmic mission to "save the Earth" can sometimes lead to what is often termed a "savior complex." This can cause individuals to feel overly responsible for the collective well-being of the planet, leading to emotional burnout and disillusionment. Alternatively, it may also lead to a disregard for the contributions of others who do not identify as starseeds, undermining collective efforts toward global betterment.

Skepticism and Scientific Scrutiny

Lastly, it's worth noting that the concept of starseeds, being deeply metaphysical, faces skepticism from mainstream scientific and psychological communities. While this book has aimed to explore various facets of the starseed experience thoughtfully and respectfully, it's essential to acknowledge that much of what is discussed falls outside the realm of empirical evidence. Therefore, critical thinking and discernment are invaluable tools for anyone navigating this terrain.

Summary

While the idea of being a starseed comes with a host of empowering beliefs and inspiring missions, it is not without its darker corners. Spiritual bypassing, narcissistic tendencies, misuse of terminology, the savior complex, and the lack of empirical evidence are all challenges that individuals within the starseed community might face. Being aware of these pitfalls doesn't diminish the starseed experience but rather adds a layer of depth and nuance that can enrich one's journey, both spiritually and practically. After all, navigating these challenges is a part of the earthly mission many starseeds are believed to have undertaken.

CHAPTER 33: INTEGRATION: LIVING A BALANCED STARSEED LIFE

While the journey of a starseed is undoubtedly filled with excitement, mystery, and cosmic purpose, it's also a human experience that requires practical navigation. For many starseeds, the earthly life can sometimes seem mundane, confusing, or even contradictory to their higher mission. Therefore, this chapter aims to provide practical advice on how to find equilibrium between your earthly responsibilities and your celestial calling.

Combining Earthly Responsibilities with Cosmic Missions

Being a starseed does not exempt one from the practical necessities of life on Earth. Bills have to be paid, relationships need nurturing, and physical health requires attention. For many, the challenge lies in integrating their cosmic missions with these earthly responsibilities.

One way to do this is by incorporating spiritual or mission-driven activities into your daily routine. For instance, if you have a strong interest in the protection of the environment and want to do something about it, you may incorporate this cause into the activities that you participate in for work or as a volunteer. If you're spiritually inclined, perhaps a career in alternative healing, counseling, or teaching could serve both your worldly needs and cosmic mission.

Work-Life-Spiritual Balance

For most people, the idea of work-life balance is already challenging. For starseeds, there's an additional layer: the spiritual or cosmic dimension. A helpful approach is to view your earthly responsibilities—be they familial, educational, or professional—as part of your larger cosmic mission.

By adopting such a perspective, you can harmonize different aspects of your life, thereby making each activity a spiritual practice in its own right. For example, you could imbue your work with a sense of service and view familial responsibilities as opportunities for soul-level growth. This way, you align your cosmic mission with earthly roles, making the two complementary rather than conflicting.

The Importance of Self-Care

Self-care isn't just a trendy term; it's crucial for anyone, but especially for starseeds who often feel the weight of their expansive missions. This includes not just physical health but emotional and spiritual well-being as well. Practices like meditation, journaling, or spending time in nature can serve as acts of self-care that refuel your spiritual energy.

Alternative healing modalities such as Reiki, sound healing, and crystal therapy, as discussed in earlier chapters, can be particularly effective for starseeds. Such practices not only offer a chance for relaxation and rejuvenation but also provide opportunities for deeper introspection and alignment with your cosmic mission.

Setting Healthy Boundaries

Given the empathic and compassionate nature of many starseeds, setting boundaries can be a challenge. Yet, it's crucial for avoiding burnout and for preserving the integrity of your mission. By setting healthy boundaries, you are not being selfish; you are actually being responsible both to yourself and to those you aim to serve.

Consider what you can realistically accomplish within the bounds of your earthly life and ensure you don't overextend yourself. Be aware of when to say no and when to retreat for rest or self-reflection. This will make your mission more sustainable in the long run.

Engaging with Like-Minded Communities

Last but not least, finding a community of like-minded individuals can offer much-needed support. In today's digital age, these communities can be physical or online. From online forums dedicated to starseeds to local spiritual or mission-driven organizations, a supportive network can be incredibly beneficial. Such communities not only offer emotional and moral support but can also provide opportunities for collaborative mission work.

Summary

Integrating a celestial mission into an earthly life is not an easy task, but it's a necessary one for any starseed aiming to fulfill their cosmic purpose while living in this physical realm. By effectively combining earthly responsibilities with cosmic missions, striving for a balanced work-life-spiritual equilibrium, practicing self-care, setting healthy boundaries, and engaging with supportive communities, you can live a balanced starseed life. This balanced approach not only enriches your earthly experience but also fortifies your cosmic mission, creating a harmonious cycle that benefits both your personal growth and the collective evolution of consciousness.

CHAPTER 34: STARSEEDS AND GLOBAL TRANSFORMATION

The idea of starseeds—souls with origins beyond our Earthly realm—has fascinated humanity for generations. As we've traversed the myriad dimensions of this subject, from their galactic origins to personal missions and spiritual tools, we now arrive at an intriguing juncture: the collective impact of starseeds on global transformation. This chapter delves into how the presence and work of starseeds could potentially reshape the socio-political and spiritual landscape of our world.

The Concept of Collective Consciousness

To understand how starseeds might influence global change, it's crucial to explore the notion of collective consciousness. This term is often described as an interconnected web of thoughts, emotions, and intentions shared by a group, community, or even humanity as a whole. When a critical mass of individuals undergoes a shift in awareness or behavioral patterns, it's believed that this transition reverberates throughout the collective consciousness, thereby catalyzing broader societal change.

The premise here is that the work starseeds are doing—be it in spiritual awakening, ecological conservation, or social justice—contributes to a shift in collective consciousness. This shift, once it reaches a tipping point, could translate into tangible changes in societal norms, laws, and structures.

Socio-Political Transformation

Starseeds often have a strong sense of justice and equality, driven by their cosmic mission to uplift humanity and restore balance to the planet. By engaging in advocacy, volunteering, or other forms of socio-political involvement, they work towards creating a more equitable world. Some might take on roles in governance, law, or social welfare to contribute to systemic change. Others may use their platforms, regardless of how great or small they are, in order to voice their opinions on important global issues such as poverty, racial and gender inequality, and climate change.

Given their inclination toward holistic thinking, starseeds might also advocate for the integration of spirituality into politics, which would be a paradigm-shifting approach to governance. The influence of starseeds in political spheres could lead to policies that prioritize collective well-being over individual gain or corporate interests.

Spiritual Enlightenment and Global Harmony

Another domain where starseeds could significantly impact is in the propagation of spiritual values like compassion, love, and unity. These values are foundational for any form of lasting global harmony. Starseeds, through their teachings, writings, or simple everyday interactions, often serve as catalysts for the deepening of these values in others.

For instance, starseeds involved in spiritual healing or teaching might facilitate transformative experiences for individuals, which could have a ripple effect on their families, communities, and eventually society at large. The adoption of these values might also decrease the prevalence of conflict and violence, leading to a more harmonious global civilization.

Ecological Stewardship

Starseeds often feel an innate connection with Earth and its ecosystem. Their efforts in promoting sustainability and ecological awareness are not just beneficial for the planet but are fundamentally tied to human survival and societal transformation. The burgeoning awareness about the intricate relationships between humanity and its environment could catalyze policy changes on a global scale, affecting areas like renewable energy, wildlife conservation, and waste management.

Limitations and Responsibilities

While the potential for starseeds to contribute to global transformation is compelling, it's vital to acknowledge that they are part of a broader tapestry of efforts aimed at social, spiritual, and environmental upliftment. No single group holds the "magic key" to global transformation. Starseeds must collaborate with other like-minded individuals and groups, acknowledging the diversity of paths and approaches to achieve a shared vision of a better world.

Summary

The potential collective impact of starseeds on global transformation can be observed across multiple domains —socio-political, spiritual, and ecological. By influencing shifts in collective consciousness, advocating for systemic change, instilling spiritual values, and championing ecological stewardship, starseeds contribute to a multifaceted tapestry of global betterment. While their cosmic background may set them apart in some ways, their earthly mission finds resonance with universal aspirations for justice, harmony, and sustainability. As part of a diverse coalition of change-makers, starseeds have the opportunity to make meaningful contributions to the unfolding story of global transformation.

CHAPTER 35: CONCLUSION: THE COSMIC JOURNEY AHEAD

Summing Up the Starseed Journey

If you've reached this point in the book, chances are you've been immersed in a fascinating exploration of the starseed phenomenon, from its historical mentions in ancient texts to its manifestation in various behavioral and psychological traits. You have uncovered the galactic roots of starseeds and delved into their missions on Earth, which range from spiritual awakening to cosmic service. Through this journey, you have gained a deeper understanding of how starseeds contribute to the evolutionary trajectory of our planet and, potentially, the entire cosmos.

Key Points Revisited

We started by examining how ancient civilizations made references to star beings and celestial entities, providing a cultural context for the modern understanding of starseeds. The exploration of star systems like Pleiades, Arcturus, and Sirius offered insights into the galactic origins of these unique souls. From there, we shifted to individual experiences, discussing the traits that make starseeds distinct from other humans. The roles and responsibilities that starseeds assume on Earth add a layer of complexity to their earthly lives, calling them to be everything from spiritual guides to ecological stewards.

Healing modalities like Reiki, sound healing, and crystal therapy were considered in light of their potential benefits for starseeds. We also touched upon how Earth serves as a kind of cosmic "school," a setting for starseeds to face challenges, learn lessons, and perhaps fulfill karmic obligations. Interstellar communication methods were dissected, enabling starseeds to connect with their star families. This naturally led to a discussion on Earth's ascension to a 5D reality, where starseeds play an integral role.

We didn't shy away from the intricacies of starseed relationships—such as twin flames and soul groups—nor did we gloss over the challenges faced by these cosmic souls in navigating their earthly existence. The use of various tools, like crystals and divination methods, came under scrutiny for their capacity to guide and energize starseeds. The book also illuminated the evolving roles of starseeds in modern spiritual communities and environmental causes.

Reflecting on the Present and Looking Toward the Future

We find ourselves at a unique juncture in history, a point where science and spirituality are beginning to find common ground. This makes the role of starseeds even more vital, as they stand at the intersection of these two realms. As humanity grapples with issues like climate change, political unrest, and a collective spiritual void, the presence of beings oriented toward higher consciousness can serve as catalysts for transformation.

Starseeds, whether they are aware of their cosmic heritage or not, find themselves amidst an increasing array of cosmic alignments, planetary shifts, and a general escalation in Earth's vibrational frequency. These conditions are not only conducive for individual awakening but also create fertile ground for collective evolution.

Final Thoughts

Whether you identify as a starseed or are merely intrigued by this cosmic phenomenon, the exploration doesn't end here. In fact, it's just the beginning. As the cosmic wheels continue to turn and the Earth navigates through an ever-expanding universe, the lessons and insights presented here may evolve. The nature of starseeds, their missions, and the cosmic laws governing their existence are dynamic, subject to the free will of each soul and the overarching cosmic plan.

One thing seems clear: starseeds have an ongoing role to play in the evolutionary drama that spans both earthly and cosmic realms. As more souls awaken to their starseed identity, it is likely that their collective impact will become increasingly tangible, shaping not only individual destinies but the course of humanity as a whole.

We've traversed a wide landscape, delving into the complexities and mysteries that surround the life of a starseed. Though many questions have been answered, many more remain. As you move forward, may your own cosmic journey be enriched by the perspectives and understandings you've gained. The story of starseeds, after all, is an unfolding chapter in the grand tale of the cosmos, one that each of us contributes to in our unique way.

THE END

Printed in Great Britain
by Amazon